AUTHENTIC

COURAGEOUS HUMANS WHO CHANGED THEIR LIVES
BY REWRITING THEIR STORIES

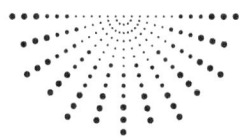

Copyright © 2021 by Dr. Tina Welsome

All rights reserved. Apart from any fair dealing for the purposes of research or private study, or criticism or review, as permitted under the Copyright, Designs, and Patents Act 1988, this publication may only be reproduced, stored, or transmitted, in any form or by any means, with the prior permission in writing of the copyright owner, or in the case of the reprographic reproduction in accordance with the terms of licensees issued by the Copyright Licensing Agency. Enquires concerning reproduction outside those terms should be sent to the publisher.

CONTENTS

WELCOME TO AUTHENTIC	v
1. April Smith Swe	1
About the Author	11
2. Bridget Aileen Sicsko	12
About the Author	23
3. Brittany Tibbitts, RDH	24
About the Author	33
4. Christine Santos	34
About the Author	43
5. Cindy Rodriguez	44
About the Author	53
6. Cinthia Hiett	54
About the Author	63
7. David Sacha	64
About the Author	75
8. Erik Symes	76
About the Author	85
9. Graham G Wheatcroft	86
About the Author	97
10. Greg Spector	98
About the Author	107
11. Julie Maigret Shapiro	108
About the Author	119
12. Kamil Shah	120
About the Author	131
13. Kristi Nellor	132
About the Author	141
14. Kristina Brummer	142
About the Author	151
15. Dr. Lesley Rivera DPT	152
About the Author	159
16. Marilucy Hernández Rivera	160

	About the Author	169
17.	Michelle Savage	170
	About the Author	181
18.	Oswald Perez	182
	About the Author	191
19.	Rachel Chamley	192
	About the Author	201
20.	Dr. Kristina Tickler Welsome	202
	About the Author	211
21.	Vicky Leon	212
	About the Author	221
22.	About The Publisher	222

WELCOME TO AUTHENTIC

Authentic comes from the Greek authentikos and Latin authentes, which means author.

We are each the author of our own life story and have the power within us to make that story a tragedy, a comedy, or a hero/heroine's epic journey. There will be protagonists, plot twists, and pivotal moments... but throughout it all, we remain the main character. It is when we come out from the dark night of the soul that we remember our inherent self-worth. That we know that the one constant in this cautionary tale is ourselves.

We are usually our own worst critics and our biggest stumbling blocks to having the life we so badly desire. It is when we realize this that we all become empowered to change the stories we tell ourselves about our past limitations, our traumas, our fears and recognize that only we can change the narrative to one of forgiveness, grace, compassion, and love for our Self and choose love over fear.

This is where our true human power lies—in being courageous to lead our lives full out with heart. This is the plot twist, where the hero or heroine makes the journey their own and stands in their true power to find meaning in their pain and triumph over it to create and live a life they love.

These courageous humans have stepped forward to share their stories of how they rewrote their own narrative to change their life to better suit their own desires. And in doing so found meaning, purpose, delight, joy, and hope. It is my wish that this hope ignites the human spark within you to unlock your own potential and create a life you love.

"Maybe the journey isn't so much about becoming anything. Maybe it's about un-becoming everything that isn't really you, so you can be who you were meant to be in the first place."

— Paul Coelho

I think we all just want to be seen, heard, valued, and appreciated for who we truly are. Unfortunately, we often deny our true selves and wear the false masks that are expected of society, our religion, our culture, our family of origin, what we think our partner wants us to be, what we think we need to be as a parent—and we tend to lose ourselves along the way. As unique and special as each one of the authors in this book are, what is common is the theme of humanity. We each have the desire to be authentically ourselves and to be the author of our own life stories. When we hear other people's stories, we find they're very relatable. It helps to make us feel less alone because we see ourselves in that person's story. And we realize that we are not the only one that thinks that way, or feels that way, or who's done that thing. The truly empowering thing about sharing stories is that as we interact with each other as humans—the courage is contagious. It empowers all of us to live more authentic and genuinely happy lives.

You too have a story. You too are the main character, the author who co-creates your story with the help of the divine universe.

When you realize this, it may create fear as you recognize that you own full responsibility for how the story progresses and ends. But when you allow love to be greater than fear, you can courageously change the stories you make up in your head. You know, the one in which you are a victim or a martyr or the oppressed? By gaining clarity and changing your perspective to one of control over your own destiny, you become empowered to rewrite your inner narrative and change the trajectory of your life.

This is a wondrous thing to behold and the life-altering experience I want for you. Join me and these courageous authors who will share their stories of struggle, learning, self-enlightenment, hope, and triumph. I know you too have an amazing tale to tell, one that changed your life and has the capacity to change others!

It's time to get clarity on your story, to recognize your courage, to use it to shine your light brighter and make an even bigger impact on the world you live in. I can't wait to welcome you to this experience!

Dr. Kristina Tickler Welsome
The Key Publishing House

1
APRIL SMITH SWE

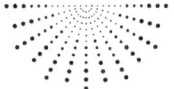

PINK BUNNY AND AUTHENTICITY

Toddling through customs in a puffy, canary yellow snowsuit covering her from head to toe, she had a death grip on a pink bunny, her sole worldly possession. When we first saw her, tears streaming down her sweet face, our hearts were both shattered and made whole all at the same time. There she was gripping so tightly to her attendant that her little fingers were a stark white against her warm brown skin. She traveled across the world to join our family. She left behind everything that she knew to go on a journey that did not feel safe for her, that was the opposite of everything she had ever known. Fear flooded her, a shrill cry erupting from her chapped, red lips. As soon as she saw the mass of people behind the plexiglass, most of whom had skin that was much fairer than her skin, her knees locked up. She turned around and reached out, begging to be picked up, to be protected from the chaos that would soon be her new life.

As soon as she walked through international customs at the Minneapolis International Airport, she would technically no longer be Eun-Mee Park from Seoul, South Korea. She would become Maya Eun-Mee Swe from Madison, WI. Her guardian would no longer be the Bo Yuk Won orphanage. She would become the third child of

Selwyn and April Swe. She would lose everything that she had ever known, only to walk into a world of perceived insecurities and dangers. While what she knew was not secure, it was predictable. She knew what her days and nights would look like. No one had prepared her, or us, for that matter, for how the actual transition might unfold.

We had it all played out in our heads, how we would change her life for the better and she would immediately become one with us. We believed that she needed us to be whole and complete, but it became clear immediately that that was not the case. She was just fine without us, or at least she thought she was. Who were we to think that we were rescuing her?

Finally, she emerged from customs, clutching her attendant with her right hand and gripping the pink bunny with her left. Now was the time for us to meet her, and she was to become ours forever. In our young and naïve minds, this would be an easy and smooth transition. That was not the case. As she approached us, we could see her trembling. She flinched at the loudness surrounding her. The big, brown, almond-shaped eyes that we had stared at in pictures for all of these months disappeared as she closed them, refusing to take in this mysterious new world that she was walking into. As we raised our sign with Eun-Mee prominently displayed on it, the attendant started walking toward us. Eun-Mee was about to become Maya and we were about to welcome our first daughter.

As soon as she was close enough to see us, we immediately rushed to hug her and welcome her home. She resisted, jerking around and bumping into the people on both sides of her. She was prepared to flee. Her attendant slowly turned her around and we approached her quickly again. She retreated again. Finally, she turned around and just stared at us. We stayed put this time, trying to read her cues. Did she recognize our pictures that the orphanage had shown her? Was she scanning us to determine if we were safe for her to approach? She stood there, hands jammed into her armpits, trying to figure out what she was going to do.

After a few minutes, that felt like a couple of hours, she released the attendant's hand and slowly shuffled toward us. As we rushed to greet her, finally, she retreated again. This little dance went on for about a half-hour. She was not coming to us and there was no way we could get to her. Starting to feel faint, I sat down in the middle of the terminal, about two arms lengths away from her sweet face, and pulled out a bag of trail mix to snack on. She immediately locked eyes with the food and started slowly, again, nudging her way toward us.

"Do you want a bite?" I asked her.

No comment.

"Here, you can have some," I say, slowly inching toward her.

No comment.

I put a couple of pieces in my hand and reached it out to her. She reached out and then again retreated. Then she moved closer, reached out, and retreated. Eventually, she took her little hand in mine and took a little bit. Then she retreated, again. Over the course of the next half-hour, she slowly inched her way closer and closer. We finally honored and respected her space and allowed her to take the reins. Eventually, she plopped herself into my lap and started digging her hand into the trail mix bag, devouring bite after bite.

Unsure what to do, we did not even know if she should eat trail mix, I leaned into her, grabbed her dirty little hand, and brought it to my face.

"Mommy," I said to her. "I am your mommy."

She looked at me, tilting her head to the side and pursing her lips, and backing away. She appeared unsure what to say or do. I locked eyes with hers, for the first time, and she immediately burst into tears. The attendant pulled back at that point, not rescuing us from this situation, and we slowly, very slowly, motioned to her to move closer. She did. And then she moved closer. And then even closer. Time seemed to stop for a moment, my eyes gazing into hers, and, at that moment, she reached out her hand, still clutching pink bunny with the other hand, and motioned for me to lift her.

"You want mommy to pick you up?" I asked, reaching down to scoop her up.

She reached up, then put her arms down, then reached up, and then back down, and then I, bending down to her level, slowly brought her to my chest. As I held her, warm, salty tears started to flow from my eyes. She felt the moisture on her cheeks and pulled back, locking eyes with me again, and then she came in and gave me her first kiss. My tears turned into sobs while her cries immediately started to dissipate.

"You're home, baby girl. You're home," I said to her, holding her tight.

Over the next hour, we have been at the terminal for well over two hours at this point, we collect the diaper bag that she brought with her, thank the attendant, and tell her goodbye. She then leans in and gives Maya a big hug, tells her that she loves her, and slowly turns away. As Maya sees her leaving, she tries to squirm out of my arms to run after her.

"Omma," she yelled. "Omma, Omma."

The attendant turned back, blew her a kiss, and kept on walking.

"Omma, Omma."

Those were the first words that we heard her say, and she said them over and over again. As she walked away, Maya's screams turned into whimpers and she eventually calmed down. We realized, in that moment, that it was just us now. Here we were, still at Minneapolis International Airport, and it was now just me, Selwyn, and Maya.

Did she even know her name was now Maya?

"Eun-Mee," I said, reaching out to bring her closer to me again.

She looked up that time. She was still Eun-Mee at that point. I do not know why we thought we could just change her name the second she arrived and expect her to respond. But we did. She continued to look at me, then look down, look at me, then look down. Suddenly, she grabbed for my red bag, where I had gotten the trail mix, and used the sign for more, more, more.

She was hungry, we realized.

"What does she eat?" I asked my husband.

"I don't know. What do you have?" he asked me.

"I mean, maybe we should go to the food court," I told him, pointing just down the terminal on the right.

Gathering up all of our stuff, we walked down there with Eun-Mee holding my right hand with her left hand, and clutching pink bunny with a death grip in her right hand. We arrive and see that there are three options. We could either get her McDonald's, Chick-Fil-A, or Red Panda.

"What do you think?" I asked Selwyn.

"Rice. We know she eats rice. Let's get her some rice and maybe some chicken?" he suggested.

"Okay, good idea," I told him. "Here, you go order and I will try to get her set up in a high chair." I then wondered, has she ever been in a high chair? Maybe we should just hold her? Let's try both and see what works.

By this point, I had to go to the bathroom, bad. I had not gone since we arrived at the airport and I could not wait much longer.

Selwyn finally got the food and Eun-Mee (she is still Eun-Mee at that point) settled, pretty easily, into the high chair. I gave her a few more pieces of the trail mix while we were waiting. Once he arrived back at the table, I told him that I had to go to the bathroom, that I would be right back.

"Are you sure?" he asked.

"Yeah, I have to go," I told him.

"Okay, do you want to take her with you?" he asked.

"No, I'll just quickly go. It is right over there," I told him, pointing to the sign.

We set Eun-Mee up with her rice, some chicken, and a few noodles, and she immediately dug in. Seeing that she was happy, I tried to slip away without her noticing.

I only got about three steps away from the table when she started shrieking, saying over and over again, "Omma, Omma, Omma."

"It's okay, honey, I'm here," I told her.

"Omma. Omma, Omma," she screamed.

"What is she saying?" I asked Selwyn. "Do you know?"

We pulled out the English-Korean dictionary and looked it up.

"Mama,' he said, "She is saying, mama."

Again, tears started flowing down my cheeks. I reached down, picked her up, and the two of us headed, together, to the bathroom.

We must have been gone for a long time because Selwyn sent someone into the bathroom to check on us.

"Ma'am, are you April?" the woman asked.

"Umm, yes, I am,' I told her, confused.

"Your husband just wanted to make sure you were okay," she told me.

"Oh, yes, thank you," I told her.

Eun-Mee and I had been playing patty cake and peek-a-boo in the bathroom stall and had, apparently, lost track of time. We quickly washed our hands and went back out to the food court.

Eun-Mee ate all of her rice, all of her noodles, and a couple of bites of her chicken. With food all over her and a full tummy, we finally decided to make our way to the car to prepare for the five-hour drive home.

Even though we brought a stroller with us and had it ready for her, Eun-Mee never once got in it. She either wanted to walk or be carried. And only by me. She was not a petite 3-year-old so I was exhausted by the time we made it to the car. As soon as we popped the locks and opened the sliding door, we remembered the little surprise that we had in there for her. Out flew 2 dozen balloons in a variety of colors. Eun-Mee shrieked, grabbed onto my leg, and would not let go. She was muttering and we did not understand one single word that she said, apart from "Omma." It took us a good fifteen minutes to console her, and pop all of the balloons to make them disappear before we were able to try to get her in the car seat. It quickly became clear that she had never used one of them and she was not happy with the idea of being restrained.

As soon as we got settled put a Sesame Street video in the DVD player, I checked my messages for the first time since we arrived at the airport. Twenty-seven missed calls, fourteen voice mails, and over forty texts. Our plan to keep everyone updated every step of the way and to document Eun-Mee's arrival did not work out so well, and now everyone was panicked.

"What's wrong?"

"Did she make it?"

"Where are you?"

"Call me. Please."

"You there?"

"You are worrying all of us, April, come on."

And on and on. I looked at my watch to check the time and realized that it was already two o'clock. We were expecting to be home no later than three o'clock. My mom had organized several of our close friends and family to be at the house when we arrived home and now it appeared that we would not make it home until at least eight o'clock. Frantic, I immediately called my mom to see what the plan was.

"Mom," I said. "Hey, sorry, the day has not gone as planned."

"Is everything okay? Where are you? Is she with you?" she asked.

"Yes, everything is okay. We are just now getting on the road. And yes, she is with us in the car right now," I told her.

"What happened? Was the plane late? You did not call. Why didn't you keep up posted?" she said, rambling and not stopping to listen to anything I had to say.

"Mom, slow down. We might have overestimated what she is going to be able to do right away," I told her.

"What do you mean?" she asked.

"The adjustment, it is a lot for her. Everything in her entire world has been turned upside down," I told her.

"What are you trying to tell me?" she asked.

"Mom, I don't know. We won't be home until eight and I don't think it is a good idea to have a house full of people," I told her, trying to break it to her gently.

"Well, I can be there, can't I? I have to be, I am keeping the boys?" she said.

"Yes, of course you can. We just can't have a party at this point. Mom, it's complicated," I told her.

I spent the next half-hour, at least, trying to explain to her what I did not even understand myself. When this process began, all we could think about was how we would celebrate our new arrival and how we wanted everybody close to us there the minute she arrived home. We did not stop to think about what Maya or, rather, Eun-Mee, might need. It had all been about us and what we wanted and needed, and not at all about her. We needed, at this point, to honor her and her needs. Yes, her arrival was exciting and we wanted to celebrate with the world. But not at her expense. Authenticity was what she needed at that time, not pomp and circumstance. The timing was just not right.

"Mom, I need you to tell everybody that they need to go home, that we will reschedule for a later date," I told her.

"What? Are you serious? There is a house full of people. There are gifts and food and drinks," she told me.

"I know. I am sorry. I really am. Mom, she's scared. She needs time to adjust," I told her.

"How about if they just stay until you get home, get a quick look at her, and then head out at that point,' she suggested.

"Mom, no. She needs us to protect her. We want her to meet everyone. We want to have a big party. And we will. Just not right now," I told her, again, as I find myself starting to get feel my chest tighten and my ears start pounding.

Maya Eun-Mee needed us to meet her where she was, not where we thought she needed to be. She continued, the whole ride home, to clutch pink bunny fiercely, with no intention of letting go anytime soon. We needed to work to be as authentic to her as the pink bunny was. Pink bunny was a genuine link to her past and we needed to slowly become a genuine link to her future.

ABOUT THE AUTHOR

April Smith Swe is a Licensed Clinical Social Worker (LCSW) specializing in crisis intervention and critical incident stress debriefing. In this capacity, she primarily assists individuals and organizations as they process and work through traumatic events. April received her B.S summa cum laude from University of Richmond and her M.S.W. summa cum laude from Washington University in St. Louis. She also has a background in research and is an avid reader.

Authenticity is key when working with people in crisis. It is difficult to create a safe environment for healing with the component is missing. As an INFJ on the Myers Briggs Type Indicator, connecting on a deeper level with people who are new to me has been a struggle over the years. It has only been by working hard to be comfortable in my own skin, and failing miserably at times, that I have developed the ability to be truly authentic in my interactions.

April lives in Williamsburg, VA and is the mother of three amazing young adult children. She enjoys traveling, volunteering at organizations close to her heart, Special Olympics, playing softball, and spending time with people at her church.

Website: www.wordshavepowertoo.com

2
BRIDGET AILEEN SICSKO

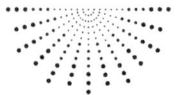

UNWILLING TO COMPROMISE

When I think about the word "authentic", I think about the aspects of our truest self that we are unwilling to compromise. And this is a story about unwillingness to compromise the aspects of myself that weren't completely fulfilled.

Not so long ago, I asked my parents "have I always had a rebellious nature?"

They shared a few examples. Once in high school I decided I would go to Germany for two years and live with a foreign family because I was craving a different experience than those around me. I had always dreamed of backpacking through Europe as my mom had done. I didn't end up going, but this was just the beginning of my desire to be me. Also in high school, I quit the soccer team. I didn't like the coach, his ethics, or his values, and something within me said, "I won't stand for this."

Looking back I probably didn't have the language or consciousness to understand what I was doing in both these situations. I was unwilling to just do what everyone else was doing. I had a desire to be different, but more importantly to be me.

This led me on a deeper journey. After healing from Lymes disease and dealing with symptoms of frequent pneumonia, parasites, and staph infections—in places where staph infections shouldn't be if you catch my drift, I already felt different in my early to late teens.

But these experiences invited me to go on a journey. And if I had known where that journey would've taken me at that time, I would have spit out my water and laughed.

Publishing, hosting a podcast, working with women around the world, and teaching yoga? I couldn't even touch my toes at the "sit-and-reach test" during gym class growing up!

But it's safe to say now that looking back, there was always a rebellious, dare-to-be-different, independent, wild-child nature to me.

It's not going anywhere.

After high school, I went on to study digital communications and organizational leadership and I quickly landed my first corporate job in NYC in advertising sales.

Cool office culture - check.

Keg machine for after-work - check.

Barista just for us - check.

Fun team happy hour - check.

True fulfillment - that left something to be desired.

About 10 months into the job, I went on a family vacation to Yosemite National Park. I remember vividly looking out at the beautiful landscape in front of me, the colors, the smells, and the shapes of the mountains. It hit me as the deepest knowing I have ever known.

"Quit the job", and so I did.

After a few more weeks of fake smiling through work, my manager began to notice my demeanor had changed and she asked me what was going on. I told her about my trip, my travels, and my interests in holistic healing.

As the coworker who would bring the chia pudding, crystals, and the latest yoga pose to work—this didn't surprise her.

Since I knew people would ask, "Oh gosh heavens, what on earth will you do?", "Why would you leave your job?", etc, I knew I needed a good plan.

I told myself, "I am going to go to school to become an acupuncturist". This ancient Chinese Medical System had greatly helped me heal during my Lyme disease journey. I knew acupuncturists made good money and it was way more respected societally than to just leave the job without a plan.

As I continued to study for my Biology CLEP exam, that was needed to apply to acupuncture school, something began to feel off.

I would start dreaming of traveling through Europe, meeting like-minded friends, exploring, wandering through new places, and learning new things. After a few months, I decided to redirect again —I'd like to call myself the Queen of the Pivot.

So here I was 23 years old, signing up for a Yoga Teacher Training at a Yoga & Ayurveda School in Ibiza, Spain. The girl who couldn't touch her toes during gym class. The athlete who said "Yoga isn't for me" and "I'm not flexible". A few months later, I had booked my entire trip to Europe, and it felt amazing.

THE CHALLENGING NATURE OF THE ALMIGHTY PIVOT

Mind you, my decisions to pivot, quit something, or divert plans completely are not always the most logical decisions. As humans, we are so used to following a set forth black and white path.

School

Get degree

Graduate

Get job

Find a partner

Buy a house

Get married

Have a baby

Retire

I refuse to live my life according to someone else's checkmarks.

For me, that "path" always felt confining and restrictive. As I write this, I am reminded of my rebellious nature. I have this deep soul yearning to do things in new and different ways.

Maybe for the sake of just being "different?"

Who can say for sure?

The beauty of my journey to authenticity and saying "sayonara" to anything and everything that doesn't serve me has been that my parents have always fully supported my intuitive decision-making.

When I quit the soccer team because I didn't feel the high school coach was being respectful or fair and I left; they supported me.

When I decided to officially leave my NYC job—they supported me.

When I decided to travel for a bit and become a yoga instructor as a career; they supported me.

There is something to be said about the nature of support. It's like in those moments when you know you are taking a freaking leap, but those closest to you are still supporting your insane and crazy dreams—magic happens.

So, after two months in Europe, I returned home with a deeper connection to my body, a completely shifted world view on what's important and I even got my period back after losing it for 2 years. Thank you, Dr. Abi, a miracle worker chiropractor who practiced Network Spinal Analysis and made some shocking connections between past medical traumas and the loss of my cycle.

I felt like layers of my old identity had died and I had gone through a massive metamorphosis. It felt good, but uncomfortable to return home to a place that only knew the "old me".

It became challenging to have old conversations about the latest reality TV shows with friends. Their gossip didn't hook me in anymore. I was craving deeper, more meaningful relationships and conversations as well as a deeper life mission.

SAYING NO

When I first returned home from my life-changing trip, I said YES to a heck of a lot of opportunities. I taught yoga anywhere and everywhere I could. I taught for free. I taught, taught, taught.

And there was something to be said for just saying yes to all opportunities, because how the heck was I supposed to know what I enjoyed if I didn't have the experience of it first hand?

I ended up getting a job working with Autistic young adults. I loved their creative minds and expanded sensitivity, plus a deep love for sound, mantras, and music. After a few months, I began feeling it was time to move on, but I was struggling to speak up for myself.

Sometimes, the Universe/God/Spirit/Source whispers but we don't listen.

Sometimes, it yells.

I got the yell and heard the clear as day signal it was time to move on after a small physical altercation occurred. No one was hurt, but we all knew it was time for me to move on.

After that experience, I started to exercise a new word in my vocabulary that hadn't quite seen the light of day in some time.

NO

NO

NO

Since then, I have said NO willingly to many, many things -- money, opportunities, "real jobs", etc.

Because when you know who you are, you are unwilling to compromise yourself even for a second.

Now here's the caveat.

This is not easy and there is lots of mental jibber-jabber that tends to float on in. You have to be able to discern between what is yours and what are the societal beliefs & constructs you have accepted as true. Aka what is yours and what is not yours. Again, that practice of discernment right there can also be challenging when there is a lot of internal banter. This is a practice I am still dancing with and every day learning to center myself with what is mine.

When you are on a path to your truest, most authentic life that doesn't look like everyone else's, be prepared to hold steady and honor that not everyone will "get it".

And if you think about it deeper, it makes sense.

Of course, someone isn't going to understand your wild decisions to leave your job and start a healing business if they have never done it themselves or seen those decisions modeled enough to know they "work".

Many people are happy living the status quo life and that is beautiful. But do not dim your light, passions, or dreams to appease their thinking of what is and isn't possible.

The path to authenticity is made for the bold, courageous, and those who dare to be "different" from the rest.

SO WHAT TRULY IS AUTHENTICITY?

How do we live authentic lives and not get caught up in the societal hoopla of how we "*should*" be living?

CURIOSITY.

I remember when I first began my coaching business four years ago, I was so surprised at something. Most of the women had never asked themselves, "who am I really?", "what do I enjoy doing?", or "how do I want to spend my time?".

And luckily, I was able to present them with a big fat permission slip that screamed, "The Choice Is Yours!".

The word authenticity requires a quest back to oneself, luckily, a quest I was able to venture down when I began dealing with health challenges from lymes disease beginning at age 15.

In a world where most of us are living by a set of predetermined rules and steps, living outside of the normal benchmarks of society can feel extremely uncomfortable and at times, lonely.

One of the keys I found on my journey to living my authentic life was finding people on a similar quest. I remember when I came home from Ibiza after my yoga teacher training and a subsequent massive spiritual awakening, I found it challenging to relate to some of my old friends. I was seeking a different type of community. I would go on meetup.com and find local meditation groups or shamanic drumming circles. I signed up for community yoga events and started creating a yoga community through my teaching. Having this group of new friends who were down to talk about crystals, meditation, personal development, spiritual experiences, our dreams, desires and connection to a higher intelligence was deeply soul nourishing.

I felt like I could be my authentic, weird, cooky, unique self. Since we were all doing some deep inner work, the fake facade that can be there in many women-only groups just wasn't there.

I realized community was a major component in my healing and I became committed to creating a North New Jersey spiritual community, since I didn't see it quite existed in the form I personally desired. I just kept listening to the call and began to host women's circles and community workshops to further my own connections and continue to make new friends. The soul nudges were apparent and I just began to listen, so find your people.

Beyond the importance of community on the "be your freaking self" journey, I also found it crucial to observe patterns, behaviors, habits and beliefs that deeply pervaded my existence, even throughout my journey to leaving all that didn't serve me.

What do I believe to be true about life?

What are some things I have done to just appease others in society?

What feels good for me?

What have I accepted as the "only way" to do something?

We have to see that we have all accepted some aspects of life as true based on our upbringing, education, family, friends, media, TV, culture, etc. But we are living in times where what is true or right for one person may not be true or right for another.

Just like in Ayurveda, there is a saying that goes, "One man's medicine is another man's poison." This is the beauty of this world, we are all different, unique, and have different "truths".

The key is to simply find what is right for you and go forth like a train moving through a snowbank — where the snow just moves in its path.

And although it can feel challenging, lonely, and at times, painful on your journey to uncompromising who you truly are, boy is it always worth it in the end.

As I sit here writing this chapter today, I can truly say that my life is one of boundaries, pleasure, fun, and enjoyment. Of course, there are the moments of the 10x soul growth and deep spiritual lessons, but being unwilling to compromise who I am for societal expectations has earned me a lot.

I am 28 years old, married to an incredible man who supports me and my highest dreams. We own a beautiful home where I get to "work" every day which typically looks like waking up around 6 am, feeding our border collie-beagle, Finn, journaling, and reading. I do my meditation, practice kundalini yoga, workout, and go for long walks as part of my "work" day. I have determined that my health is just as important as sending work emails and facilitating my masterminds and networking calls. The rest of my day is spent recording for my podcast, where I get to have the richest, deepest conversations with leaders from all over the world, writing emails, posts or prepping content, having calls with my support team, dreaming about the books I want to produce, spending time in my garden and cooking our homemade meals.

As I look back on my journey thus far, I am grateful for my willingness to stick to my guns and let what is meant to come, come and what is meant to go, go. My childhood rebellious, "I don't like to follow the rules nature" has provided a pretty clear path of entrepreneurship where I get to brainstorm new business ideas that honor different ways of doing, being, living, and experiencing life.

It is my highest hope and intention that this chapter serves as an initiation of what is possible for you when you set forth on a journey to live as your most authentic self.

You will surprise yourself again and again as you begin to see, listen, notice, and take action upon the little internal soul nudges that have always been there.

You begin to say "heck yes!" to the things that make your eyes widen and your heart warm.

And you begin to say "no, thank you" to the opportunities and invitations that just don't feel like you.

And although you might have some naysayers on that journey; I can promise you it is one that you will never regret or forget.

ABOUT THE AUTHOR
BRIDGET AILEEN SICSKO

Bridget Aileen Sicsko is the founder of Exalted Publishing House, a Podcast Host and Visibility Coach. She helps successful entrepreneurs standout and be featured as a leader in their industry through sharing powerful stories. Her mission is to amplify the voices of powerful entrepreneurs who are ready to elevate their business, become published authors & public speakers. Bridget also hosts a podcast called "The Gathering MVMT" where she has interviewed over 60 entrepreneurs, TedX speakers, authors, thought-leaders, & visionaries who are here to uplift humanity. Bridget has been featured in Women's Business Daily, Authority Magazine, Medium, Thrive Global as well as Ticker News and News 12 New York.

Website: www.bridgetaileen.com
Email: bridget@bridgetaileen.com
Facebook Community: www.facebook.com/groups/rockthemiconline
Instagram: www.instagram.com/blissfulbridget
Podcast: podcasts.apple.com/us/podcast/the-gathering-mvmt/id1546684870
Linkedin: www.linkedin.com/in/bridgetsmith8193/

3
BRITTANY TIBBITTS, RDH

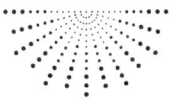

ELLE POTENTIAL

You can fully step into your power, unlock your full "she" potential, embrace your full femininity

.. AND still, be taken seriously.

I remember the day vividly. I was sitting in my car on my way to work. I had to be there by 6:45 am, if I wanted to have 15 full minutes to get my operatory set up and prepared for my first patient. They were expected to arrive at 7 am. In the dental profession, it's essential to be mindful with every minute of your day. Patients are set in the schedule, so time management is critical to your success for staying on track. Patients are scheduled one after another and you are only allocated a certain amount of time for each appointment.

I was at a red light and I remember looking at the car in the lane next to me. As I sat there, waiting for the light to turn green, I wondered what the person in that car did for a living. I fantasized on the idea that they were not married to a fixed schedule that offered no type of opportunity or flexibility like I was. I pictured them being able to drive in their car mid-day, mid-week, should they please. As much as I loved serving my patient base, my soul CRAVED for this flexibility and freedom. The idea of being locked into a set schedule with no allowance to pursue other opportunities of the day was soul-crushing. Don't get me wrong, I was a proud dental hygienist who strived every day to provide comprehensive quality patient-centric care, but my heart and soul desired more. I wanted to broaden my reach. Expand my impact. Create room where I could flow throughout my day versus my current rigid regimen. I desired for expansion and growth beyond my current practice setting.

The light turned green, and my thoughts started to pick up as fast as my mph. It was in that exact moment that I realized how stagnant I felt in my profession. I became aware that if I wanted this freedom, that I so badly desired, serving as a dental hygienist in my current capacity was not going to allow me that. Aside from strengthening my clinical skill set, upward growth was not the usual structure of the profession -unless I went back to school and became a dentist -which was of no interest at all to me. I adjusted my rearview mirror, in hopes that I would see the answer of how to bridge this gap from my current reality to my future dream. As I looked into the reflection, I realized I was trying to find my new destination on a path I was already driving on.. in autopilot. My posture quickly stiffened. I knew that if I wanted to make this change, I would have to take a new, unfamiliar path. I envisioned my current route becoming a past path traveled.. and suddenly the reflection in my rearview mirror became the familiar sight of my current reality.

I pulled into the parking lot of my office and sat there for a moment, looking off into a blurry distance. It was in that very moment where I had to acknowledge my truth. I desired growth and expansion so desperately. I wanted to have a broader impact and influence. While I loved my patients, my ambition wanted to take me past the walls of my confined operatory and into a larger arena. These thoughts were so loud they could no longer be ignored. I began to feel sparks of inspiration start from my head and pulse their way into my heart.

This inspired passion was streaming into my veins. There was more for me out there and I knew it. The time was now; I needed to own this truth and take action. I knew I had so much unknown potential ahead of me and if I wanted to tap into my power, I had to take the first step.

I had the experience of working in a wide array of practice settings; privately-owned offices, corporate-owned offices, specialty practices, and even working as an on-call hygienist for a temp agency. Clinically, this profession does not offer a lot of opportunity for rising within the practice setting. When I first started in the dental industry, the typical structure was that the dentist was a male doctor who owned his practice and had a team that comprised, in most cases, of women. Growth or expansion was nearly impossible. In most situations, the manager of the team was the dentist's wife. As time progresses, the profession is evolving and this dynamic is shifting.

At this point in my career, I was practicing hygiene in a corporate setting. Luckily, corporations offer many growth opportunities beyond the clinical setting. I began to quickly realize that no one was going to advocate for my growth. If I wanted to rise, I needed to throw myself into the arena. I needed to start taking the initiative to position myself where my value was seen beyond my supervising dentist and patients. I was eager and hungry to learn and connect with other professionals of my industry. As soon as I became aware of this and set the intention to grow, I started to see everything through a different lens. Every action I took was out of intention and fueled by my passion; it was inspired action.

I found that the more I started to believe in myself, the bolder I became at taking action and calculated risks. Confidence and courage became the foundation that I needed to house my conviction. Once I did this, I was able to pivot away from any self-doubt and stand confidently in my power to move forward. The funny thing about growth and expansion is that it requires you to take a different action than what you once were previously doing to obtain different results. Rule of thumb; You must step into a new way of thinking, to step into a new way of being. This school of thought was important because I realized how I needed to shift my identity in a new direction. My challenge here was that the new path outline was not mapped out. There was no blueprint telling me how to get from point A to point B. I didn't want this anyway. I made "safe" moves my whole life by listening to the direction of others.

My growth journey required me to shift my mindset about any roadblocks that prevented my forward momentum. If I wanted to make progress, I would have to relentlessly charge through any uncertainty, doubt, or challenges and trust myself as my compass. I learned to see obstacles as opportunity-packed challenges, which became necessary to achieve serious strides forward. In order to face any challenge head on, one must believe in their ability to overcome the challenge, so strongly, that they can pivot away from any self-doubt, and into their power. I learned how to do this, but it was not easy. I remember when I first started in my profession. There were times where I would work with a doctor and they would respond to my ideas in a condescending tone. This profession gave the doctor more credibility for their knowledge, and rightly so. However, it can be argued that this also promoted a dynamic and climate where the doctor took advantage of this professional hierarchy, lacking social graces and crossing professional respect boundaries. Please understand not every doctor treats their team like this. However, it does occur and you can imagine how this would create an intimating environment. It did not allow or promote team members below the doctor to feel confident to flourish. You could even argue that it did not offer the team an opportunity to grow. Who would want to step into their power, if you were afraid your idea would be knocked down or that your knowledge was not valid or held any substance?

Being a young female, this was intimating and took time to overcome. It seemed to overlap in my personal life too. As I reflected, I realized how I always just flowed through life, but in a way where I let the current direct me. I was navigating through my life without intention or accountability of ownership. I didn't realize this though. I thought I beat to my own drum, made my own decisions, and lived a life designed by me. In those moments, I might have thought I was, but clearly, I allowed and let others persuade my journey. I never challenged or questioned the societal flow of life. I couldn't see through the projections that my loved ones and friends had laced within their opinions and advice. The beliefs and opinions they shared were intertwined with their own fears and insecurities, based off of their own past experiences. We each create our own limits based on this and when we share our guiding words, we don't realize that our projections are also wrapped up in them. I am now super aware of this and take every opinion with a grain of salt. I do not allow it to have a huge influence on my direction.

I was a recovering good girl who, up until this point, did what was expected of me, in a way where I did not want to rattle any waters. At the time, I thought I was living life according to my own design and terms. Truthfully, I was just living docilely. The pivotal point for me was when I had my very own awakening. It was as if all of a sudden I realized that I had been wearing rose-colored goggles my whole life and had just become aware that I actually had the right and ability to take them off to see life through my own clear, unfiltered lens. This became evident when I went through a major life event that would throw me off my current course, knock me down, and make me look at this directly in the eyes. When you look your problems, old belief systems, and even generational patterns in the face and see them for what they truly are, your desire becomes strong to want to start putting the work in to take different actions to get different outcomes. The problems become highlighted. They scream so loudly that you have no other choice but to address and work through them.

To overcome this, naturally, you need to believe in yourself and stand strong in your truth. I have found great value and benefit in building up my own confidence to give myself enough self-belief to fuel and act on my faith and convictions. This is how I battle self-doubt internally or externally. Whether it be from myself or doubt projected from others. As my confidence began to grow, so did my opportunities. I was able to take any challenge thrown my way and transform it into an opportunity to learn and to grow. When you approach everything from this perspective, you become more empowered to take bolder action. This became the cycle that led me to transition from the clinical care setting and propelled me into new arena's, where I would evolve into new roles. The more people I worked with, the more I noticed a repetitive common pattern. Before anyone can truly thrive, they need to battle away from self-doubt and strengthen their confidence so they can stand firmly and boldly in their power. When you do this your impact also strengthens.

I would go on to mentor and coach dental health providers and professionals across the East coast. I created leadership programs that helped impact the quality of care patients were receiving by building up the confidence, knowledge, and skill set of the dental health professional. As I started to see the positive impact I was having, my curiosity and desire to expand my reach only strengthened. I started to throw myself into new arenas. I wanted to sit at the table with the big decision-makers. I did not fit the part though. I was a twenty-something year old female who had been in the industry for just about five years. My ambition wanted me to claim my seat at the table, which comprised primarily of men who made all the decisions for the corporation. I knew I would not be invited at the table, but I also knew there was a seat there waiting for me to claim. Instead of waiting for the opportunity or invite that I knew would never come. I started showing up to the shareholder meetings as if I was meant to be there. I dug deep internally to tap into my confidence and knew there was one thing left to do. I had to invite myself to the table. The moment I did this, I was not shut down. Instead, I was welcomed to sit. My first few meetings I observed with little commentary. I am a big believer that you must get a good bearing and understanding before you can effectively contribute. Each meeting, I found myself leaning more and more into my power, wanting to contribute, and started to vocalize my ideas. My ideas were not warmly welcomed, but remember I had worked hard at this. I knew my convictions were solid, I knew I had ground to stand on and that the information and ideas I possessed were of value. When I talked, I talked with conviction and confidence. This is how you capture influence.

As my confidence strengthened, each step I took became bolder. I was becoming more daring. I trusted myself, my convictions, my faith and believed strongly in my goals. I was no longer afraid to speak up or put myself out there. I wanted to become visible for the purpose of having a positive impact. I am addicted to the growth journey and committed with putting myself out there to make positive strides forward. I don't believe you can take any missteps on your journey. Every experience has meaning and purpose behind it. When you move with inspired action you are open to any outcome. You have a strong inner knowing that you were urged internally to do something because it is part of the process of leading you closer to your goals and dreams. I want to fall; I want to make mistakes. Each step is a step in the process. It is not about perfection; it is about progress. Sometimes progress has more meaning internally, rather than externally. Use the challenges as tools for your toolbox. They will serve you in the future as an experience that you have learned from and will be able to guide you to take the right step forward, based on the lesson that the experience had previously taught you. The more I stayed loyal to my convictions and in alignment with helping others along the way, I became unstoppable. I knew how to navigate myself through the journey. The thing about the growth journey is that you have to have a defined goal in mind, but the map which will lead you there is not always clear. You need to take every step with confidence and conviction.

It was a huge shift but I found myself going from novelist dental health professional in a male-dominated industry to the director of operations. I was running the professional corporation just over five years into my career at this company. My desire to grow is strong and this is only part of my story. I would go on to face further challenges and greetings of resistance in other areas. Striving to continue to grow was a challenge as I transitioned from the clinical arena and into the operational arena. I went from overcoming a male-dominated setting in the clinical aspect and into a male-dominated operational setting in the corporate aspect. Overcoming this experience has influenced my desire to help women navigate through similar challenges they face in their profession or personal lives. I help women unlock their potential, pivot away from self-doubt, and step into their full potential. As women, we can fully embrace our full femininity and be taken seriously.

ABOUT THE AUTHOR
BRITTANY TIBBITTS, RDH

Brittany Tibbitts RDH is an author, speaker, mentor, coach, entrepreneur, and founder of Elle Potential. She has successfully climbed the corporate ladder throughout her career. She is a licensed dental hygienist, which has enabled her to excel in both the clinical and operational settings of her profession. In her first five years, she learned and mastered clinical care within her scope of practice and business operations, found her voice, and claimed her seat at tables dominated by men. Her experience has allowed her to mentor and coach hundreds of dental health students, providers, and professionals, as well as lead affiliates as the Director of Operations in the Northeast. Through her experience, she learned how to step into her true authentic power to unlock her full, "she" potential. She has achieved both personal and professional success by overcoming barriers and passionately believes in helping other women step into their power to make this possible for themselves.

Instagram: https://www.instagram.com/brittanytmarie/

4
CHRISTINE SANTOS

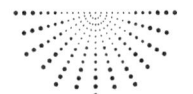

MY HEROES AND RESILIENCY

I looked up from my desk at the far end of the classroom to see my brother dressed in his state trooper uniform standing in the doorway. I knew...

I was four years old when my father came to visit us for the first time after sending us away. By this time, we had moved twice since my now little family of three left my birthplace of Milwaukee. We were living 1000's of miles away from my dad in a quaint little home. It was on a nice street, and we had a front sitting porch and a fenced-in yard with a playset. There were three bedrooms upstairs on the second floor where I did most of my playing. I had a nice small bedroom with a slanted ceiling, painted all white with a bureau and bed and enough room for me to play between them as well as in the alcove of the room where the ceiling met the floor. I had a window that faced the street, and I would often sit on the edge of my bed, looking out the window.

It was so much nicer than our first home away from Milwaukee, where we lived in an apartment on the second floor of a tenement. Where our neighborhood seemed scary to me, and so did the kids that lived next door. I only have two memories of that first apartment, one was when a dog came onto our porch from across the street, and my cat that was on the porch with me got scared, so I picked her up and in fear, trying to get away from the dog she scratched up my face, blood poured down my face as I screamed for my mother. I still have the scar next to my eye. The other memory is of when I had a pet frog that I loved. I had found him outside and decided to keep him. I had him for a couple of days and would take him with me outside. I loved him so much. I was walking past our neighbor's house with him in my hand, and the kid on the porch asked me what I had. I told him it was my pet frog, and he asked to see him. I went over to the stairs and put him down on his step. The kid stood up and stomped on him right there in front of me. I remember his guts coming out of his mouth. I ran back home crying.

Shortly after that, a house became available in a nice neighborhood that we could afford. I was excited to have our own house and backyard to play in. This quaint home was one of the last places I remember being with my father.

I don't remember the specifics of the visit, but as far as I was concerned, one of the last significant memories of my father was during this visit. You see, I thought he had come to take us back home. But what unfolded in mere minutes was the exact opposite. He was leaving without us. When I realized this, I was determined to change his mind. I grabbed his leg as tight as I could as he stood in the doorway, begging him not to leave us.

I remember his pants and the feel of them, soft yet precise and like "home". No matter how tight I held on to his leg, and no matter how loud I screamed for him not to go, he didn't respond. He didn't say anything or even touch me. Then it came to me, and I knew what I needed to say. I screamed as loud as I could, "I'LL BE GOOD!"

I gave it all my might. I felt like I was crumbling to pieces right there in that moment. He finally responded by prying me off his leg and choosing to leave. I failed. I failed at keeping him there for me, I failed at keeping him there for my mom, and I failed at keeping him there for my brother. How could this be happening?

I ran to my room; my play space and my sanctuary. I would never be the same.

From that moment forward, it was the three of us making our way in the world. My mother and my brother, my two heroes.

In the early years, we lived in that quaint home, my brother and I played together, and I played in my bedroom a lot. My mother worked multiple jobs at a time to make ends meet. My brother and I would be home with babysitters, and whenever she was late coming home, I would begin crying, thinking she had died and was never coming back. I always thought she had died in a car accident because I knew in my heart she would never leave us. So many nights I would be crying in fear that she was gone. I would go to her room and hug her clothes in her closet, crying until she finally came home.

We didn't have much money, and I knew my mother worked so much because we needed the money to live in that house and have food on the table. So, we, of course, never went on vacations or even rarely went anywhere on a family adventure. But one time, my mother took my brother and me to the circus. I was excited and mesmerized by all the sites. There was so much to see and take in that I became distracted and wasn't paying attention to follow them, and when I turned around, my mother and brother were gone. I was petrified. I started crying and found a woman working at a booth and told her I was lost. She didn't respond. Then I decided I would hide in the bathroom to stay safe. As I was heading towards the bathroom, my brother found me. I was so relieved and felt that he saved me. I hugged him as tight as I could.

One time while playing in my room, my brother and I decided to play a glow-in-the-dark game, so we went to my closet that had a spring lock on the door and were playing the game in there. I got up to go to the bathroom, and when I came back, I pulled on the door too tight, and it locked from the outside. We were locked in my closet. I began to scream and cry and started throwing things at the door. Nothing seemed to work to open the door. I hugged my brother and told him that I loved him. I thought we were going to be stuck in there forever. As so many times before my brother came to my rescue, he stood up and kicked the door open. We were free!

My mother and my brother were my everything, and I knew they would take care of me.

One day we found out that we would have to move from our house because the owner was selling and we didn't have the money to buy it. We went from that quaint little home and my room to an apartment on the second floor of a tenement in a tough neighborhood. My mother continued to have to work a lot to make ends meet, and my brother and I were home alone most of the time.

When my mother was at work, people would call the house, and when I'd answer, they'd tell me they knew we were home alone. I was so scared. When I would ride the bus to school, the other kids on the bus would throw their cigarette butts at me. Yes, in those days, middle schoolers were allowed to smoke on the bus. To me, the other tenants in the house were scary, the neighborhood was scary, there was no backyard, and so my brother and I stayed in the apartment all the time.

During those years, we would occasionally see my father. Once or twice he would visit, and we would spend some time with him. By this time, he was a stranger to me, and I certainly didn't understand him. He had remarried, and his wife had other children, one who was around our age would occasionally come when he visited. I certainly didn't understand why he got to be with my father, live in a nice home, in a nice neighborhood, and not be scared all the time. I, of course, didn't know any of this really. I just imagined that was what their life was like where they lived. I was always under the impression they had more than enough money, and we certainly didn't.

The years passed, we moved a lot, my mother continued to be our rock, keeping us safe. My brother went off to bootcamp, and I missed him so much. He would write me letters, and I always loved hearing from him.

Then one day we received a call that my father was ill and it seemed that he didn't have much time left. There were a lot of conversations around us going to see him, whether it was the right thing for all three of us to go and stay in his home with him and his wife. And then, of course, the fact that we couldn't afford it. I certainly wasn't sure if I wanted to go. I was in my first years of college, no longer living in scary neighborhoods, no longer feeling as if I was going to lose everything at the mere stomp of a foot or my mother coming home late. I was busy living my college life.

I had never been back to my birthplace or visited my father in his home. I wasn't sure how I would feel if it would be too hard to see where I could have grown up, what my life might have looked like, and to see my father, now certainly a stranger, knowingly for the last time.

Close friends of my parents kept in contact with us over the years. They were the family I always wanted us to be. A mom, a dad, and two children living in a nice home and neighborhood, with money to take vacations and have nice things. When they heard my father was ill and we knew he wouldn't have much time left, they offered to pay for us to fly out to see him.

I wondered how I would feel returning to my birthplace. Would I feel a sense of belonging? Would I feel a sense of sadness, as perhaps a life that should have been mine?

With the generous offer from our friends, the decision was made. My mother, my brother, and I were going back to where we once lived to stay with a man, my father, who we barely knew, and the wife and family he had spent his life with.

As we were landing, I looked out the plane window, wondering if I would start to have a sense of home, and as we drove to his house, I looked at the landscape and neighborhoods searching for a feeling of belonging. When we got to his house and saw him, he looked so ill all my thoughts and wonder about our surroundings disappeared. I knew I was looking at a man that was going to die. I knew I was looking at my father preparing to leave me again.

His doctor came to the house to talk with all of us. I remember we sat around the living room with my father, who was so frail and sick, and his doctor telling us how much they had done and tried, and there wasn't much left to do. He was dying. I can't imagine how this could have felt for him, hearing about his impending death, surrounded by strangers who shouldn't have been strangers.

We stayed a couple of days in his home. He didn't make any attempts to sit with my brother and me alone. We had dinners with him and his wife, just as if we were unfamiliar guests in his home. There were no meaningful conversations or questions answered.

I looked at it as if he was leaving us again. And again by his own doing. He had drunk himself to death—another choice he made, which to me didn't make sense.

On the last day, as we drove away from the house, he stood in the doorway and watched us drive away. I wanted to stare longer, knowing I would never see him again, but it felt strange that that would show an emotion that wasn't reciprocated

In the days that passed after our visit, I was on a sort of an exhilarated high. I felt a sense of strength, a sense of knowing my family, my heroes, my mother, and my brother; we had all been through a lot together over the years. My mother had worked way too hard, holding down multiple jobs, we lived in terrible situations, I was scared a lot of the time, yet we persevered. I felt as if I could choose to make my life the way I wanted. We had been through some really hard times. And all those years, I wondered what my life would have been like if my dad had wanted us to stay together as a family. But, it didn't matter because the three of us were strong and resilient together.

Going to see my father facing that unknown was an incredible culmination and realization of the strength and resilience we all had. It was incredibly hard. I felt bad for my brother and my mother. I felt badly for my father. I felt sad knowing I would never get any of the answers I wanted over the years. Why had he decided to send us away? Why didn't he want us to live near him so we could be close? Why didn't he come to visit more often? Why did he let us live in such terrible places and situations? Why didn't he love me?

I knew now for certain I would never have those answers. What would that mean for me? What effect would that have on my life? Would I forever be broken? I had imagined one day, when I was older, I would reach out to him, he would welcome me with open arms, and we would have those conversations. I would ask all my questions and get all the answers I wanted and needed. I knew then this would never be the case. More importantly, I knew I never wanted to make the choices he made. And I knew I could decide to be happy, and I could decide to work hard and make a different life for myself. I could choose to be resilient and move forward and not rely on a someday when I would get all my answers. That day would never come, and I saw that it wasn't needed to live a happy life.

Yes, I would never be the same, and I would be stronger and more intentional about my choices. And I certainly knew I could get through hard times. I felt different, I felt resilient, and loved by my heroes.

As I sat in my accounting class, I looked up from my desk at the far end of the classroom to see my brother dressed in his state trooper uniform standing in the doorway, my mother behind him crying. I knew...

The breath left my body for a moment, I paused, my brother and I locked eyes, and for a moment, nothing else existed around me. I became extremely aware of the situation. I didn't want to get up from my seat. I knew as soon as I did and I started to walk toward my brother and mother, it would all be over. There would never be the answers, and there would never be a chance to have the love of a father. I waited, probably longer than I should have, and then finally I got up...

ABOUT THE AUTHOR

CHRISTINE SANTOS

Christine is a leader, mentor, speaker, certified life coach, author, podcast host (Wonder Boldly), on-line course creator. She started her business in career coaching but has pivoted to coaching women entrepreneurs; helping them form daily practices and long term visions so they can perform at their best.

She coaches women entrepreneurs to put themselves first to build a strong mindset. She does this through her signature program Harness Your Morning and providing group and 1:1 coaching. She is an expert in Positive Mindset, the host of the Wonder Boldly Podcast, and creator of the Harness Your Morning Program. She brings her unique perspective from being a leader in corporate for over 27 years. Her success is founded on a positive mindset.

Website: www.drizzleacademy.com/
LinkedIn: www.linkedin.com/in/christine-santos-63307234/
Instagram: www.instagram.com/christinebsantos/
Podcast: podcasts.apple.com/us/podcast/wonder-boldly/id1512274383

5
CINDY RODRIGUEZ

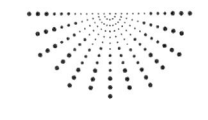

SOUL ON FIRE

Nine years ago, on a blisteringly hot day in Africa, I walked into a simple one-room sewing college. Each girl was standing barefoot, singing, swaying, and clapping their way into my heart. My soul cracked wide open in those moments where passion found me in Kenya.

When the singing quieted, there was a moment of pause. They stood tall, and I just soaked in this feeling of being seen. It wasn't awkward nor fleeting. While I hadn't anticipated going there, it was exactly where I needed to be. With each passing moment, I could feel my body exhale. The music had cut through all the layers and we just saw each other in the raw. Pure beauty was flowing.

As humans, we inherently crave being seen and heard, and on that day, it felt exhilarating to have both happening at once. Those initial moments of exchange created this bubble of feminine energy, and I felt open and safe as I began listening to their stories. When the translation began from Swahili to English, I recall floating in and out of disbelief. The context of modern-day child brides, female genital cutting, and the repetition of the voiceless experience in each story was difficult for me to digest. One underlying theme that tied all their stories together was that when you are born on the remote soils of Kenya, it is undoubtedly one of the world's worst injustices.

I could feel the protector in me rise as the girls shared their afflictions. Questions swirled in my head...Why is this her fate? How is this only a plane ride away from America? What are her human rights? I looked for words of comfort, but my voice was stuck in between a space of shock in what I heard and a feeling of powerlessness. Tears just flowed, and I felt my own story surface without being able to put words to it yet. Simply put—in Her, I saw ME.

I wanted to protect these girls, but also looming was this feeling of wanting to escape. I was ashamed to feel that way, but I was processing so much at once. With a simple gesture directed at me, it was my turn to share my story. I blurted something about my family background, and then I paused. This time, I did not want to be seen nor heard. This shocking surge of shame surfaced from the pit of my stomach up to my throat. The spicket of being vulnerable had been opened—for her and me. All that was left was to make the choice of sharing my truth. So, the words spilled out messily.

I surrendered to the shame I felt with the shadow side of being Mexican-American. It was such a conflict for me to admit that (and still is) because it has taken me decades to own the power of being a vibrant Latina versus hiding it from the world so I would not feel the wrath of others' prejudices. By being brutally honest with myself that day, I unlocked the cage door, but I wasn't quite ready to fly.

The human experience that unfolded led me to this truth: The day I met those girls was the day I met myself.

I felt...

alive.

Connected.

And generous.

I gave a piece of my soul in that little one-room sewing college, and in return, I felt activated. It was not random. It was no mistake. I was simply open and utterly present to an experience I had not seen coming. This gift of meeting her had flowed into my life, and I was ready to receive it, fueling all my cylinders with female empowerment. I was fired-up to uncover a way for us both to impact change and left with a gut feeling that we were both being given a second chance to reclaim ourselves.

When I returned to the United States, I began Elimu Girls and started a 501C3. Elimu means education in Swahili. Our mission is to give her a voice, a choice, and a bank account through a two-year sewing and boarding program. Elimu Girls lead the charge for change in their communities by transforming themselves into entrepreneurs and role models. They walk out of the program and into an elevated position in their families that can dramatically change their fate. Knowing that I can reach even just one more girl gives me deep meaning and purpose. The *why* behind the work I do is razor clear to me, but the *how* is what started this next challenging phase of my life. The one where I begin to reclaim who I am and define who I want to be.

As a new leader of a non-profit, I was all heart with little business savvy. I was confronted with growing a new business and full of entrepreneurial ideas when I found myself blocked. My desperate desire to help the Elimu Girls forced me to dig deeper into why I felt paralyzed. I got curious and began to learn more about myself. I worked to discover why there were moments where I struggled with the duplicity of feeling powerful yet shameful. I had never dared to say this out loud before as I was not self-aware enough to even understand what was happening on the inside, much less give it a label. My parents raised us not to be ashamed of who we were, but there were prejudices and circumstances beyond their control. I felt a new magnetic pull to be more Latina, but my life was steeped in American assimilation.

When I looked into the eyes of the Elimu Girl, I also saw those of a young Mexican woman staring back at me. Her story was one of a patriarchal system that positioned her as a second-class citizen, where she struggled with confidence and worthiness. This deep connection to her allowed me to understand that she was attached to invisible strings—ones that were heavily tugging on her and holding her in place. But what were they? What were the levers that made her story and my story resonant? I began to arrange this puzzle of feelings in my own life.

FAMILY HISTORY AND MY GROWING YEARS

My family is Mexican-American, and the experience of prejudice and assimilation were woven into our lives. At times, I felt the sting of direct discrimination myself. And other times, it was witnessing my Mexican community in Los Angeles being marginalized.

Let's go a bit further back for context...In 1930, my father was born into America's largest brickyard settlement in Los Angeles, called Simons Brickyard #3. Hundreds of low-cost family dwellings were built by the owner, Walter Simons, for his recently immigrated Mexican labor force. The town functioned in a silo with its own school, market, church, social hall, and even its own baseball team. William Deverell credited my grandfather in a book called White Washed Adobe. He mentions that Carlos Arnold was strong as an ox and a man who could do anything. My family was poor, but content living in this protected brick-company town.

During the great depression, there was raging racism and resentment of Mexicans infiltrating the job market. Signs across the USA read, "No dogs, Mexicans, or Blacks." Outside the Simon's gates, Mexicans were being illegally deported back to Mexico in accordance with President Hoover's Repatriation Program. When Simons Brickyard #3 closed, life radically changed for my father and his family. The safety net of being protected in a town with invisible ethnic borders had dissolved. He was thrust into a world of survival in a segregated school system that echoed to many Spanish speaking Mexican-Americans that they were "less than." The racial divide of Mexican-Americans was prolific.

Similarly, my mom was from an unincorporated mining town that skirted the edge of Death Valley. Named for the chemical used to make soda-ash, Trona, was an attractive company town for many Mexican workers looking for employment. My Grandpa, Modesto Garcia, moved his family from Los Angeles and made a new life in Trona, CA. But even amongst desert living, the racial divide was thick. My mother's family lived in an all-Mexican neighborhood segmented by the Trona Railway Tracks. Grandpa was working in a plant that operated 24/7 but was told that he would never advance higher within the company because he was Mexican.

These experiences shaped our family history. The hardships fueled my parents to raise five strong-minded children. Both having lived with racial segregation, they believed that education was the key that would unlock this inequity— along with straight teeth and assimilation practices, which included not speaking Spanish. My dad was my world growing up. He is a man of deep integrity, and I would go to the ends of the Earth for him. My mom is one of the strongest Mexican women I know. She is spiritual beyond words. Together they raised their children to rise above the prejudices that were beyond their control. They laid the foundation for my success, but we all know that everyone must find their own way.

And so it was.

With my last name being Arnold and the skin tone of Snow White, assimilation seemed easy. I witnessed how the world treated Spanish-speakers and felt the stares when Spanish was spoken in public settings. This embarrassed me, and I would sometimes feel "less-than" so I actively chose to dim my brownness to gain a sense of belonging from the outside world. I frosted my hair blonde, straightened my natural curls, and learned to speak English with formality. Even though I felt the pull of the Latina force in me, I quieted that voice so I would not stand out.

It pained me to understand this paradox of not being "Latin enough." When I would be amongst my Latina friends, I was teased, "Gringa" (Spanish term for white girl), or "Arn-eo" (Arnold + Oreo implying brown-outside, white-inside). There was a sassiness in this banter, but also a notion that I wasn't white, and according to some good friends, barely Mexican. I was frozen between two worlds.

I focused my time and energy on my education and had found success quickly as a school principal. My love life took a backseat to a thriving career for many years until I agreed one day to go on a blind date with an accountant. Yes, an accountant. What in God's name would an educator and an accountant talk about? As I sat at El Carmen's, a scrappy tequila bar, not knowing what to expect and terrified that it was going to be one painfully boring night—in from the rain, walked this tall, stylish, gorgeous Latino man full of enticing energy and confidence. I was magnetized by his wit, and with each passing moment, I fell in love with his quick mind, spirit, and openness to possibility. The conversation never once fell to numbers and spreadsheets, not the kids I served. After hours of laughing, storytelling, and absorbing all of his positive energy, I knew we'd build a magical life together. I had no doubt, and thankfully neither did he. I found the love he had for his Latin culture to be a signed permission slip for me to go full-Latina and 18 years later, I love to see that my children have embraced this as well. The Universe delivered this life-changing gift to me in the form of a friend and partner who celebrates my duality and invites further exploration. He is slow medicine for me.

My career aspiration as a principal was to be a superintendent and grow the scope of helping students of color. But this was overshadowed by two things; I did not love the political aspects of the public school system, and I could not impact change fast enough. I was itching to keep expanding my destiny and my purpose. Then one day, an opportunity presented itself to work with teachers in Kenya. I leaped. I was scared but did it anyway because there was a force inside of me that said, "Hell-Yes." I went on the trip to work at Upendo Nursery School, but my heart found its way across town to that one- room sewing college. It was my destiny to meet HER, the Elimu Girl, and find myself along the way.

Spirituality has been the next area to unfold in my life. It's still in process, but I strive to live from a soulful place and know thy wounded-self. As the Founder of Elimu Girls, I used to operate from a space of being her protector and wanting to save her, but this approach has evolved as I have embraced knowing my wounded parts. I am grateful for this new, feminine leadership style that is full of intuition and emotional intelligence. It is this space of sharing my wounds and vulnerability that allows me to help her. We are one in the same, and our wounds are universal to our gender and the color of our skin.

My son recently said to me, "Did you know you never see your own face?" It seemed simple enough when he said it. But he made me think... I can literally see myself in almost everyone I encounter, especially the downtrodden. I don't feel any division amongst women as we face the world together. We are linked arm in arm. She rises. I rise. I know now *that* is what drew me to the Elimu Girl. That is what gave me the courage to explore my own journey. It is what allowed me to continue to find my voice, even when it feels shaky. It has guided me to learn to love all the parts of me (even the parts I loathe) and to be able to share my evolving story.

I invite you to loosen the buckle and begin to share your story. You have one. And I bet it is powerful. It is the only way to invite true authenticity into a conversation. We have limited days on this Earth, and you might as well toss the ego, let in the magic, and just go for it. You don't have to go to Africa to find that you can be a force for good. We all have an Elimu Girl staring back at us, and the question is: What will you do? Will you let your guard down and connect? Can you empower those around you by being vulnerable? Will you be generous with your story? Courageous with your words? Will you stand in your power?

I believe you will.

We are limitless when we pour service into one another and believe in the power of one. We can move mountains, and the tribe will follow because they pick up on our energy. That energetic exchange is contagious. Each of us can ignite an inner fire that drives purpose and meaning, but it is the genuine connection with another soul that enables us to be powerful beyond measure.

ABOUT THE AUTHOR
CINDY RODRIGUEZ

Cindy Rodriguez is a second-generation Latina woman living in Southern California. Her family stories chronicle the lives of the poor Mexican immigrants who worked at the Simons Brickyard in Los Angeles, CA. She feels a sense of connection with the poverty-stricken teens in rural Kenya, as they were both given a second chance at life through education and empowerment.

Cindy is the founder of Elimu Girls (a division of Elimu-USA), a 501(c)(3) established in 2013 to equip girls with the skills to transform the outcomes of their lives. Her passion for human rights and gender equality led her to start this grassroots international organization. She's a former teacher and administrator with an MA in Curriculum & Instruction and an MA in Education Leadership.

Her life's mission is to help others ignite their inner fire that craves purpose. The power each of us hold for profound impact is immeasurable.

Website: https://elimugirls.com/
Instagram: https://www.instagram.com/elimugirls/
Facebook: https://www.facebook.com/elimugirls

6
CINTHIA HIETT

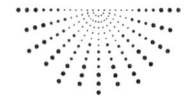

CAN FAIRYTALES BE REAL?

Stories. We all love them, don't we! Stories inspire, they challenge, they teach. Stories allow us a peek into someone else's life and let us walk in someone else's shoes, if only for a brief moment.

As far back as I can remember, I have always loved anything alive - from animals to reptiles, to bugs and birds, and especially humans. I can fall in love with people very quickly and deeply enjoy getting to know them. It is rare for me to spend time with someone and not attach to them. It usually happens very quickly and people feel the same connection with me. This is not to say I do not have good boundaries. I just care very deeply and very compassionately. I love getting to know people. You see, every human is truly so unique, complex, and sometimes, maybe, very complicated.

People frequently say to me: "I can't believe I told you that, you're so easy to talk to". I would oftentimes hear what great insight I had, and "how did you know that without me telling you"? "I feel like I've known you forever." The obvious assumption might have been that I would gravitate toward a profession in healthcare, ministry, psychology, coaching or teaching, as it came so naturally to me. I did finally land in the healthcare industry and was a licensed psychotherapist for over twenty-five years, and recently retired my license to do coaching and consulting. However, it became very apparent at a very young age, that "I" felt incredibly compelled to follow a different path. As I reflect on my own life story, I realize I have had three stories going on in my life simultaneously, kind of like a braid. The first story is the reason why I'm here—the supernatural story that's bigger than me, the one that the Creator is unfolding in my life. The second story is the story I'm writing with my choices in life. And the third story is my fairytale, it's based on imagination, fantasy, dreams, aspirations, and escapism.

So how have these three stories played out in my life?

They began with the hope of my fairytale story. You see, I was adopted and although I had Christian parents that loved me and cared for me, there was always something missing. As a little girl, I fantasized that I was secretly a princess that had been misplaced or lost. I dreamed that my real family was desperately looking for me; and when they'd find me, we would all live happily ever after.

I always knew I was adopted, and even though my parents handled my adoption very well and always worked at making me feel loved and wanted, but being very different than my adoptive family affected me greatly as I was growing up. My adopted parents attempted to make clear how very much they wanted me; how long they waited for me, and that they specifically picked me. They always considered me their "real" daughter. I would like to say I was convinced, but I was so different than them and felt that they wanted a child more like themselves. I interpreted their lack of enthusiasm for my interests and talents as rejection and judgment against who I really thought I was. As a result, I felt they were not interested in the "real me" and would only love me if I was "like" them. What I have come to find as an adult, is that my parents were very aware of my gifts and talents but were concerned about my future, and what that atmosphere and lifestyle may do to me. To that end, I know they loved me, and still love me very much!

Being raised in a Christian home, I always heard how much God loved me. I would like to say that knowing this truth fixed things for me. But somehow my feelings of rejection, abandonment, not measuring up, and struggling to figure out "who I was" and "who I was supposed to be" became very problematic for me. I knew inside of me that I felt one way, that certain things came naturally to me, and that I was very different than my family.

This difference was revealed early on by the fact that both of my parents were very intelligent and highly educated. My adoptive mother had a Master's Degree in Education and was the president of the school board at the school I attended. My adoptive father was an extremely introverted and gifted electrical engineer with top-secret government clearance. He designed the power converters for Voyager with NASA and this satellite is still sending pictures. Needless to say, they placed a great deal of importance on education.

Though I was intelligent and considered gifted, all I ever wanted to do was sing, dance, act, or perform. Singing, cheerleading, gymnastics, swimming, and modern dance all felt so familiar, so perfect, so "me." All the while, my parents continuously asked me, "What about your education?" I would respond back with, "Why do I need an education, I'm going to be a Rock Star"! I didn't care; I just wanted to perform—I just wanted to sing. I was featured as a soloist on a record my church produced when I was 6-7 years old, and sang the same song on television. I was not nervous, I loved it! It came so naturally to me. The more often I was asked to sing whether it be on television, at events, in musicals, in show bands, etc., the more convinced I was that this was what I was meant to do! This was my fairytale, which I was going to make be "My Story." It was a very painful journey for my parents and myself, probably for God, but I wasn't really interested in a religious experience.

I barely made it through high school with a "B" average, and college was no different. I couldn't get out of my home fast enough. I wanted to be independent and to spend my time doing what I wanted to do. I started dropping classes at my university because I would rather sing, perform, and play music. My parents were beside themselves.

One fateful day I had an "ah-ha" moment during band practice when I realized the "band" was probably never getting out of the garage. It was clear we most likely weren't going to "make it". I humbled myself and went to my parents and said, "Well, I don't think the band is going to "make it". I guess I'll try college again? My father looked at my mother and said "What do you think she can do?" My mother replied, "Well, she likes the Mall"!? I finally got it together enough to pick a major: fashion merchandising. At least this was a Bachelor of Science degree. I thought this degree was creative enough to satisfy both my parents and me. I was accepted at Northern Arizona University. I moved up to Flagstaff, promptly joined a sorority, became the Chaplain, and joined a rock band. In retrospect, it is very telling, as I became an ordained minister in my thirties. I truly thought I could continue working on my singing career, my life's dream, and please God and my parents.

In the last semester of my senior year, I felt a spiritual nudge or maybe more like a shove! The manner in which I was raised began to compel me to look again at my faith and spirituality. When I was little I had made that decision to be baptized. However, as an adult, I stopped relying on God because I felt like I had a pretty good "gig" going on my own. This was now "my story". I kept dreaming that it was my destiny to sing. More and more, though, I was feeling conflicted about my relationship with God and wasn't sure if I wanted to open the door to spirituality again? I told God that He would have to "convince" me he had a better plan.

Of course, He did, and I must say, to His credit, He was quite polite about it. However, It still took a while before I fully recognized the work he was doing in my life.

"My Story" continued after graduation when I accepted a job as an assistant buyer for Robinsons–May in California, with 21 stores from Santa Barbara to San Diego, and was driving a little white Porsche 924 with a sunroof! Life couldn't be better, right? Wrong. I was miserable. I was in a bad relationship, stressed out, and hated my job because it was all numbers and orders, nothing creative at all. Even though I was successful and promoted at work, all I wanted to do was sing. Just like high school and college, all kinds of different people would say to me, "I heard you were great to talk to, can I tell you something and see what you think?". The employees, department managers, even the store manager would seek me out to run something by me, telling me I had such great insight. Or ask, "What do you think this means, what do you think I should do?" I worked for a major cosmetic company and was considered one of the best in the SW region. My managers didn't realize the sales numbers were off the chart because customers would schedule weekly makeovers in order to sit and talk with me about their problems. They would subsequently end up buying makeup to legitimize how long they sat spilling out their story. While I looked like I had it together on the outside, my insides were a very different picture; I was depressed, anxious, overwhelmed and empty.

It was only then that I came to find out God's Story for me. You see, we rarely accept or look for God's Story unless the fairy tale doesn't work out, and "our story" seems to be failing as well. Let me tell you, He convinced me—through trying and failing to do it on my own—that life without Him would be a nightmare. I mean, really—I thought I could do better than God? I finally offered my life to God, and He so graciously accepted it, even though I had categorically messed it up. All I had to do was ask! Let me tell you, It was quite humbling to say:

"God, do you still want my life, the way it is, and what I have done with it?"

I got a resounding, YES! You see, God wasn't waiting for me to "get it all together." He was actually waiting, patiently and kindly, for everything to fall apart. I came to learn that God wants me at my best **and** at my worst. I started going back to church and became very involved in the music and led yet another band doing contemporary Christian music. I thought to myself . . . Ohhhh, God wants me to be a Christian Rock Star"!

However, some of the problems I'd brushed under the rug for years were coming to the surface. Earlier in my life, I had experienced sexual abuse and coupled with the deep feelings of abandonment and rejection from my adoption, I developed an eating disorder that began in high school and continued through college.

I was so self-conscious about my weight. I always felt fat and felt like I couldn't "live" this way. What was so tragic is that I wasn't "fat", I just grew up into an adult woman, with a "women's" body later than other girls. But I went from being the tiniest cheerleader as a freshman to one of the bigger cheerleaders as a senior, growing 6-7 inches the last two years of high school. People took notice and were not very kind. I've always been a very sensitive artistic type, and as a result, the eating disorder continued to dangerously worsen leading to hospitalization and treatment.

Sometimes the best things happen to you when you're in such a dark place you are unable to recognize it. In the treatment center, the psychologists and doctors continuously remarked at what great insight I had about psychological methods and causation, as well as a deep understanding of the other patients. After a month of treatment, I was released and at the time I believed I was healed. I began speaking, doing commercials, and doing personal testimonials about the dangers of eating disorders; all the while I continued to struggle with food, fear of getting fat, and struggling to do the "right thing". This created a terrible paradox for me because I didn't feel like I could tell anyone I was still struggling. I was supposed to be "healed"! Eating disorders are very tricky and insidious. You can't just "quit" eating like you can quit alcohol or cigarettes. What was amazing is how God worked these things together for my good. I found that I loved psychology and psychotherapy. I began to integrate self-care, and decrease hatred and judgment toward myself. I worked in several treatment centers for eating disorders, teenage drug addiction and alcohol abuse.

What felt so miraculous was that I kept getting job offers for positions I was not yet qualified to take, based solely on my reputation and personality. I continued to hear in each facility "you are such a natural at this, can I run something by you?" Several times I had to clarify that I didn't have my Master's Degree yet or my certification as a psychotherapist. Yet, in one job after another, God paved the way and I was able to see patients and work on my master's program simultaneously. I began to "see" how serendipitous these "opportunities" were as doors just seemed to open for me at inpatient, and outpatient treatment centers. I was able to develop programs, trainings, and eventually landed in private practice. I would speak and educate groups and professionals on the intricacies of eating disorders. I was able to do many testimonial appearances regarding eating disorders and would include singing to help, inspire and encourage those who struggled with eating disorders, or the loved ones of those who were struggling. Truth be told, I loved the work, and felt honored to be a part of healing people's lives, however . . . I still wanted to sing and perform.

God's story for my life has proved to be a far better story than I could have ever written for myself, or even fantasized about. I am able to do such creative work in healing people, helping them accept and honor themselves, find their true reason for being born, and see them thrive. I have produced several musical CDs, some of which are my original music.

In spite of all my bad choices and trying to make "my story" work, God still wanted me. There was still a reason I was here - still more to be discovered and uncovered.

My story has come full circle in the last couple of years, as my husband researched, searched out, and found my biological family. When I saw a picture of my biological father, it was the first time in my life I actually looked like someone. It's impossible to describe what this felt like. I finally looked like someone! I came to find that both my biological parents were performers. My mother was a modern dance performer and traveled the nation dancing. My father was a very accomplished and successful musician and author. His mother (my grandmother) was a concert pianist. My favorite instrument has always been the piano. It has been incredible to meet my half-siblings and I look like them! We share many of the same talents, abilities, and temperaments.

Neither of my biological families knew anything about me. My half-sister told me how skeptical they both were when my husband contacted them. She remarked by saying, "I told my friend she looks like dad and has done everything dad has done. I was born in the early 60's, and people were not forthcoming when "illegitimate" pregnancies occurred. I continue to see more and more throughout my life the supernatural presence which I call God being so kind, accepting, flexible (thank God), and loving. I must say I have not always felt this way. But I am thankful and grateful for my life—something that has taken years to achieve. The biggest takeaway from my life experience is realizing, accepting, and acknowledging that I am a "one-time-occurring" person and there is a reason that I was created. No one can succeed in the ways that I can and no one can fail like I can. I want to leave this world better because I was here.

I believe our truest story is the one we live when we participate within God's story for us. Our fairytales are intended to give us hope and vision. They give us the energy to continue to "walk out" the story God has for us—it's bigger than us, not a copy or re-make; it is our unique imprint on this world that cannot be undone, redone, or counterfeited. If there is one thing I can impart, is to embrace your uniqueness, to be "the best version of you", touching the world in a way that only you can, good or bad, knowing . . . the world needs you!

ABOUT THE AUTHOR

CINTHIA HIETT

After living life on her own terms, following what she'd thought was her ultimate dream, Cinthia Hiett hit rock bottom. In her chapter, *Can Fairytales be Real?* Cinthia illustrates what happens when you shift from following your "dream" to stepping into your higher calling.

From this perspective, Cinthia has built a successful career helping others discover who they truly are and understanding how to become the best version of themselves. Cinthia is a life coach, author, podcaster, and motivational speaker with over 30 years of experience. Her education includes a Master's Degree in Counseling and Hiett has taught the Psychology of Religion at Arizona Christian University among other courses. Cinthia is widely recognized as an international speaker who shares inspirational and relevant teachings and presents biblically-based seminars and lectures on relationships, gender and conflict resolution.

Website: www.cinthiahiett.com/
Instagram: www.instagram.com/cinthiahiett/
Podcast: apple.co/3uhHW8p
Other Books: www.cinthiahiett.com/shop

7
DAVID SACHA

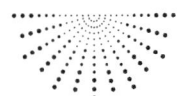

SELFLESSNESS: THE FEAR OF LOVING YOURSELF

Selflessness— The sign of a good, loving, and moral person. It's often never questioned when we see someone who gives themselves to others. Living that ideal used to be the core focus of who I wanted to be. I spent much of my time working to be mindful of the world around me. I wanted to be mindful of how others thought, felt, or hurt. I worked to love without expectation. What I didn't realize was that I had completely lost myself. My identity was centered around, instead of enhanced by, the act of helping other people. This manifested into a fear of being selfish. A fear of putting myself first. A fear of being heard. A fear of loving myself.

The catalyst to overcoming these fears centers around a relationship with someone who is no longer in my life. The fallout of this relationship is what allowed me to look inward and acknowledge what I was going through.

BEGINNINGS

I met Brandy freshman year of college. The more we came to know each other, the more I felt this was someone I could truly be myself with. I felt safe with her and we shared the same humor. I realize now, she was someone I could be vulnerable with in ways I hadn't been before.

We dated throughout Freshman year, then over the summer, she broke up with me. I was devastated. I felt I lost something I would never find again. Additionally, I felt I had lost an essential source of emotional support. I told myself I was okay with simply being friends with her. This seemed better than not having her in my life at all.

I began constantly trying to "prove" myself in the hopes she would see my value, change her mind, and come running back to me. That 'thing' we had is what I was holding onto. Everything became about getting that back. This felt easier than allowing life to bring me to something new.

Over the next two to three years, we would be on again off again friends. By the time I graduated, she had cut me out of her life five times. Often left wondering why. I feel her reasons weren't based on anything I had done.

At one point she accused me of stalking her. I ran into her outside of the school's woodshop and she mentioned not remembering where her car was parked. I had seen it when I drove into work, so I told her where it was. She became very aggressive and asked if I was stalking her. I didn't understand why she would say that; it just wasn't true.

Brandy was quickly teaching me the relationship we had would always be on thin ice. That at any given moment, I could potentially slip up and she would immediately cut me out of her life. Constantly feeling this way hurt.

This mindset forced me to scrutinize every action I made towards her. "Am I reading into this? Will this come off as overbearing?" Whenever she came back into my life, these types of thoughts were constantly running through my mind. Whenever I did notice something, I would tell myself, "She's just being nice" or "We're close friends, don't overthink it." I was terrified of her reading into something. I felt all I could do was suppress my feelings to the point I didn't even know if they were there or not. I felt I couldn't risk scaring her away again.

One instance that deeply hurt me, was when a girl at our school spread a rumor I was prowling around the school library, hitting on women and making them feel uncomfortable. Not only would I never do that, but I had only visited the school library when it was absolutely required for class. I barely had time for my homework, let alone to bother women in the library. Those who know me would attest to the fact this doesn't sound like me.

When word of this got to Brandy, she confronted me about it. I defended myself, but that wasn't enough for her. I told her if she didn't believe me, then there was nothing else I could say and perhaps we shouldn't talk anymore. After that, I received no response from her.

The next time I heard from her was November. Brandy came to me with a letter when I was working in the woodshop. In it, she apologized and explained her actions. She was adamant she didn't expect a response, and if she never heard from me again, she would understand. She also expressed how important our friendship was. This dramatic approach was consistent whenever Brandy wanted to repair the relationship.

My boundaries were porous and I still wanted her in my life. I always forgave her because I was happy to have her back. Deep down, I knew it was because I hoped she would finally see the value in me. I wanted her to think, "Wow, no matter what I do, David cares enough to hear and forgive me." I know now I was only fooling myself.

My forgiveness was a sign of my codependence on my relationship with her. She could do no harm. At least no harm that could permanently end our relationship. By having no real boundaries, I was showing her I would always be there no matter what she did. I needed her friendship and was dependent on it. I'm patient, so I was willing to wait for it to come back.

POST-COLLEGE

A month after the letter, we fell out again and didn't talk for a year. We reconnected as seniors and stayed friends for the next two years. During the six months after I graduated, we would hang out and things felt normal. I believed I had genuinely reached the point where I wasn't seeking anything more.

In November of 2017, my internship was coming to an end and it appeared my contract might not be renewed. I reached out to a supervisor from a previous internship and he felt my talents were best suited in California.

Later, when I received the official news my contract wouldn't be renewed, I had no idea what I was going to do. 24 hours later, I received a text from my previous supervisor saying, "Do you want to fly to California next week?" I couldn't believe it. I had lived on the East Coast my whole life, and here I was on the brink of a new adventure out west.

I took the opportunity and left for California. It was a one month contract with the potential for more. When I returned to Cincinnati for Christmas, I used my first paycheck for a downpayment on a car. Then drove up to Detroit to show it to some friends and spend New Year's Eve there. Brandy was one of those friends and we agreed to meet for lunch.

As far as I knew, I was simply meeting a good friend for lunch. What I didn't know was that moving to California brought some things up for her. I had previously mentioned to Brandy, I was planning to hang out with another female friend the next day. I could tell this bothered her, but I didn't understand why considering the narrative she had given me about our relationship. "Why would she care? She had told me she wasn't interested in me.", I thought. From my perspective, it was well established she only saw me as a friend. I noticed she was asking a lot of questions about her. Then she said, "Tell her that you're already spoken for."

I was blown away— This was it. This was the thing I had waited the past 4 years for. I asked if this meant she wanted to be in a relationship again and she said it did. I expressed hesitance since I was going back to California. I did the long-distance thing in high school and was not a fan. This felt different though. In my mind, with over four years of knowing each other, we could make this work.

Without giving it a second thought, I told her I wanted the same thing. "What could go wrong, right?" This is what I wanted and now I could have it. What more could I ask for?

We dated for 4 months and she broke up with me. I'm not unsympathetic as to why she broke up with me— I became distant and pushed her away. But I had my reasons. At the time, I was pursuing a long-term contract at a company I would work with for the next 2.5 years. It was a start-up car company, so I wanted to dedicate as much of my time to it as I could.

I have always felt people and life are more important than work. So I was confused when it seemed easier to focus on work instead of her. If this was THE person, why didn't I want to dedicate more of my time to her?

Here is where my mental space was at the time. The last two months of the relationship I felt her old patterns were beginning to show. She began accusing me of being materialistic, a show-off, and many other things. All of this made me afraid to bring up anything good that was happening in my life out of the fear it would upset her.

Something else that upset me was I noticed she didn't trust me. My best friend Dennis moved out there to work at the same company as me. Naturally, we were having our adventures. Brandy felt unappreciated because I was either busy with work or hanging out with Dennis.

The reason I wasn't prioritizing her was due to the lack of trust she had in me. I thought, "Why am I putting effort into someone who is constantly second-guessing me and has no faith in me at all?" My doubts were further validated after a situation that came up when Dennis and I went to a local bar.

Dennis and I walked in and there were 2 girls sitting at the bar. We sat near them and the bartender immediately started to wingman for us. At some point during the conversation, they wanted to add us on Instagram. Since I had no intention of pursuing anything with either of these girls I saw no harm in adding them.

However, in the back of my mind, I wondered if Brandy would notice. Not even 30 minutes later, I received a text from her asking why I was adding girls on Instagram. I was livid. I felt the text didn't even justify a response because I knew I deserved more credit than that. I felt intensely disrespected by this. I shouldn't have to constantly notarize every interaction I have to appease someone's mistrust in me. Especially since I've never given reason to warrant such mistrust.

I felt my actions over the last five years were more than enough to earn the kind of trust that says who I am can be relied on. Her distrust was pushing me further away from her. If she had waited for me to explain to her what happened that night, I would have told her about the ridiculous incident that came up at the bar.

Instead of laughing over this silly situation, she's angry because I rightfully ignored her intrusive text message. Not long after, she broke up with me. I was beginning to remember her true colors.

At this point, I was simply tired. Tired of the back and forth. Tired of waiting for her emotions to settle and then months later coming back with an apology. Tired of feeling unheard and misunderstood. Tired of feeling like my point of view wasn't being considered, despite my constant effort to see things from her perspective. I've been through five years of this now and I've had enough.

After breaking up, I promised myself I would never date her again. This would be the absolute last time I let her do that to me. Short of a complete and total personality change, I wouldn't break that promise to myself—at least that was the ideal.

POST-BREAK-UP

Two months after we broke up, she reached out and we began talking again. I felt that since we were not in a relationship and she was in Detroit, there wasn't any harm in remaining friends.

Brandy enjoys writing poetry and often posts it on her Instagram. Over that summer, many of these poems were about me. I knew this. However, I chose not to read into it or listen to her words, because I wasn't ready nor did I want to go down that path. A fact she would later hold against me.

My feelings remained the same till November. On November 1st, 2018, early in the morning. My sister, Kristin, died of an untreated UTI infection. There is a lot I could say about this, but I feel it's a story better saved for another time. The reason this is relevant is that Brandy drove down to support me. At the time, her presence meant the world to me.

The emotions surrounding this tragedy had me second-guessing the way I felt. Before she left, I told her, "My sister's passing has me reconsidering everything. I feel I might be overthinking all of this." She seemed receptive to this. I felt I was taking life too seriously and I should start dating her again. However, I told her I needed a little more time.

A month later, she was understandably tired of waiting. Later on, she mentioned that at this point, she had lifted her feelings for me up to God. A couple of weeks after we had plans to hang out for New Year's

Eve. During this visit, I noticed more distance from her and a closeness growing between her and a former friend of mine. A friend whom I used to confide in when I was struggling with my feelings for her.

Upon returning home and talking with this friend. I realized the possibility of them dating was becoming inevitable. This caused a five-year emotional cork to pop in me. Suddenly, every emotion I was suppressing rose to the surface and it hurt like nothing I've ever experienced before. For a week and a half, my body was in a fight or flight mode. I felt this was my last chance to express everything I've ever felt towards her. My last chance to be heard.

HEALING

Looking back at messages, I noticed I became willing to compromise every aspect of myself in the hopes it would open her eyes. My words would fall on deaf ears. I feel she could only see things from the perspective of the past year. Anytime I tried to expand the context, she would completely dismiss it or change the subject. Refusing to acknowledge or listen to it.

As I was trying to explain to her how I truly felt, I started remembering the horrible ways she's made me feel. This gave me the courage to defend myself. In doing so, it forced me to look at the last 5+ years from a more objective standpoint. Each message I sent her revealed more things to me. Each message became less about "getting her back" and more about being heard and acknowledged for what I went through.

By having a hard and painful look at our relationship as a whole, I began to see the truth. This experience allowed me to finally acknowledge that over the last five years she had been emotionally abusing and gaslighting me. I loved her, but I did not love myself enough to know I deserved to not be treated this way.

This was a hard reality to accept, but I knew it was true. However, I wanted a second opinion. In the past, I believed therapy was a great thing, but that it was a great thing for other people. I do my best to be mindful because every story has two sides and it's generally unfair to assume your side is faultless. So I decided to seek out a therapist to help me sort through the debris and figure out what was on my side of the street. That got my foot in the door. Since then, therapy has become an essential part of my life.

BE SELFISH

The biggest lesson I took from all of this was to love and not lose myself. A big part of love is understanding. To me, this means learning to understand and grow through the aspects of myself I can improve on. I've since learned of my codependent and avoidant tendencies. This knowledge has completely changed the way I see myself and has taught me how to set boundaries. To quote one of my favorite comedians, Daniel Sloss, "If you only love yourself at 20%, that means someone can along and love you 30%. You're like, 'Wow, that's so much!' It's literally less than half."

Love yourself at 100%. I now believe that it's essential to be selfish if you want to be selfless for others. Without this, you run the risk of losing yourself in other people. Your value becomes dependent on how others see you, the amount of 'selfless' value you bring to other people, and it demonizes taking care of yourself.

Have the courage to be selfish. Put your mask on first when the plane is crashing. If your ship is sinking, how can you help other sinking ships? Fix your fucking ship and then you can bring others on board and take them to safety. You gain nothing by sinking your ship with the rest.

While trying to care for other people, learn to care for yourself along the way. Doing so means knowing when to ask for help. Seeking help doesn't mean you're weak, nor does it mean you're a burden. If you struggle with this, the hardest lesson will be accepting that saving everyone isn't your job.

"There is nothing wrong with being selfish for a bit, because you have the rest of your life to be selfless." -Daniel Sloss

Selfishness is so often painted in a negative light and understandably so. However, nothing is ever black and white. Life is full of exceptions to rules and that's part of what makes it beautiful. We are constantly learning of the new shades between black and white. Embrace them.

ABOUT THE AUTHOR

DAVID SACHA

"David Sacha (pronounced SHAH-kuh) is a passionate and driven individual. He's the co-owner of Akton LLC, a digital design consultancy. He's also an artist, dancer, and a persistent seeker of growth.

In his chapter, David discusses a journey that awakened him to his fear of self love. Since then, therapy, friends, and new experiences, have helped him rewrite his story.

David attended an all-male Catholic high school where he was required to go on a three-day retreat called Kairos. This retreat was a safe space for young boys to express emotions; many for the first time. He later returned to lead and share his own story with classmates and teachers. Looking back, Kairos was essentially group therapy. Kairos taught him the importance of vulnerability.

David, now 26, uses what he's learned to help other men express emotions. He's does through his @man.i.feel Instagram where he publicly shares his feelings.

Website: https://akton.blue
Instagram: www.instagram.com/djshocka
www.instagram.com/man.i.feel/
Email: davidsacha@akton.blue"

8
ERIK SYMES

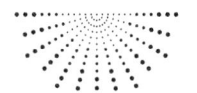

CONFRONTING DEPRESSION WITH AUTHENTICITY

The last thing I've spent a significant amount of time embracing in my life is authenticity. That is until recently. The last half of 2020, well really the last three and a half months of 2020, became a sort of personal renaissance. In life, we all endure struggles in one form or another. It is simply part of the experience. We are, after all, human. Contending with depression has been my struggle. If I'm being honest, denying and hiding my depression is a much better way to describe the experience than contending with it. For any of you reading this who have dealt with depression, know someone who has, or simply knows anything about depression then you might understand that depression is the nemesis of authenticity. Additionally, depression usually teams up with shame and that's a powerful combination, keeping authenticity in the dark, buried somewhere deep inside. But I learned something about shame over those last three and a half months of an epically bad year, which was shame also has a nemesis and its name is vulnerability. Without vulnerability, it's almost impossible to embrace and put your true authentic self on display. Vulnerability acts like a light that shines, allowing authenticity to find its way to the surface. This is exactly what I want to talk about - the shift that can occur if you're willing to open up, be vulnerable, and expose your true authentic self.

My first experience with depression came in the mid-90s, after giving up on being a professional artist, specifically a graphic designer, and spending too many years in a series of unfulfilling jobs through the 2000s. I never had a career, just jobs. I told myself that was "fine" because most people just have jobs and most people are happy with that, so therefore I should be happy with that. Of course, I didn't know that to be the case, it was the story I was telling myself so I could "get over it". I rationalized that by accepting work that was not in any way creative, I was being noble - doing "the right thing". It was 1994 and I was getting married in six months. I needed a steady job with some assumed stability. I had bounced between a few short-lived jobs where I was utilizing the BFA in visual design I had earned in 1991, but the jobs were scarce in the early 1990s. I worked as a layout artist for a national magazine but was the victim of downsizing. I landed a job as a junior designer at a small firm, but it turned out they just needed me to complete a project and seven weeks later I was looking for work again. Finally, I ended up at another small firm specializing in communications and public relations, which would've been ideal if I had more experience and some confidence in myself. This probably won't come as any surprise to anyone with an understanding of depression, but I've struggled with confidence and low self-esteem since I was a kid.

So, I found myself stocking shelves at a grocery store. This was the job that got me through college but certainly wasn't supposed to be the job that was my only source of income nearly three years after graduating. I had friends who were doing well in the design field at this point, and I started to feel ashamed of myself. I began questioning my talent and ability. Feeling ashamed, coupled with the fact I was getting married soon, was all I needed to convince myself that I wasn't good enough to make it in the design field so I should just forget about it and get a job, any job. Not only did I tell this story to myself, but I became convinced it was true. Negative self-talk took hold of me and became my de facto inner dialogue. I began to wallow in negativity, cynicism, and pessimism. It eroded what little confidence in and respect for myself that I may have had and spiraled me into some dark places.

Just prior to getting married, I took a job as a computer operator for a software company that licensed tax software for municipalities in Massachusetts. This bears repeating; I was a *computer operator*, which I'm pretty sure isn't a thing anymore, and was the complete antithesis of art. What I was doing every day for work was anathema to my very being. I worked there for over six years in two different roles, later as an account manager. Not only were the jobs unfulfilling, there was the added benefit of it being a toxic workplace. My peers were great, but the owners were belittling, devaluing, and hypercritical. They had this pseudo high school clique mentality. They would put people down behind their back and sometimes right to their faces. I didn't recognize it at the time, but depression was settling in. The inner self-talk that I had developed got much worse, with very little positive messaging regarding people in general and the world at large. There was even less positive messaging about myself. With each passing day, I was becoming nothing more than a façade. My wife at the time and I had friends, took vacations, and spent time with family. We did things that were fun. Vacations were especially fun because I felt like I was escaping the reality I had created. But even when I was having fun, I still felt worthless inside, like I had no value. I didn't believe in myself. I was ashamed of what I had become. I couldn't talk about how I was feeling, so I started to pull away and shut down. With friends, I learned how to appear happy, but I never gave too much of myself. I kept things superficial and people at arm's length. The less people knew, the better. It was exhausting keeping up appearances. Going to work every day was exhausting too. I had to because, like everyone, I had responsibilities and bills to pay. After work, I had little interest in anything other than lying on the couch and watching TV. The most exercise I got was walking our dog, which I preferred to do alone. I became increasingly negative, cynical, and hostile. The shame spiral sped up and took me deeper, because I wasn't willing or able to talk about how I felt.

By August 2000, I reached a breaking point with work and left for a new job with a different company. I didn't even bother to look for work in design, because I once again convinced myself it was too late and I was too far removed from the field. This new job was also with a software company, and I worked there from August through December 2000. Then I found a job at a major global high-tech company, hoping that a higher salary and advancement opportunities would give my life some meaning. I started January 2nd, 2001, feeling optimistic for the first time in a long while. Shortly after I started, the trickle-down effect from the "dot-com bubble burst" began to affect business and there were layoffs. I kept my job, but morale was low. Then 9/11 and more layoffs. Once again, I kept my job, but morale sank further. My team of 18 people dwindled to 4, managing the same workload. What optimism I had was gone. The inner-self talk told me this was all I was worthy of. I was even more withdrawn than before and started having suicidal ideations. The most prevalent came as I was driving home, thinking how easy it would be to put the gas pedal to the floor and drive into a bridge abutment. Shame was keeping me from admitting my feelings to the people in my life that mattered the most. It was destroying me and my marriage for nearly eight years.

Even though I drank socially before, now I was numbing myself with alcohol and I was making a lot of bad financial decisions because it allowed me to feel something that wasn't horrible for a moment or two. I leased a pickup truck knowing full well our budget was tight. I remember taking a cruise where we nearly ran out of spending money. All transactions were billed to our cabin - the final bill would not come until the last day. I was drinking too much and buying drinks for others. I got concerned about the bar bill, so I requested it just prior to the end of the trip, and it made me feel sick. I had to cut back my spending to avoid running out of money and keep anyone from finding out. I paid the bills, so I hid it all until I couldn't anymore. I started getting a lot of calls from creditors. Self-medicating through unnecessary purchases no longer felt good and just added anxiety to the equation. This really should've ended the marriage, but it lasted a couple more years until she couldn't handle my behavior anymore and left.

I was faced with telling my family and friends that my wife had left and that I had been struggling with depression. They were all supportive including my soon-to-be ex-wife, which didn't surprise me but didn't help allay my shame. I started seeing a therapist and taking Prozac. The fog I was in lifted. I felt genuinely good, which was a foreign feeling. At this time, I didn't understand why I was depressed. My shame prevented me from being vulnerable, I withheld and didn't open up. The funny thing is that you don't get anything out of therapy if you aren't willing to truly examine yourself. My outlook was that the Prozac made me feel good, ergo I was good. I wish antidepressants came with the clear instruction that they don't fix you, only you can fix you - actually, I prefer to say heal. I don't believe people are broken and in need of fixing, I believe people are wounded and in need of healing. An antidepressant will certainly help lift you out of a depressed state, but if you don't commit yourself there's a very good chance you'll relapse. You have to "do the work". I didn't do the work, but because I felt so much better, I convinced myself that I had. I continued to use Prozac as prescribed for a few years, but what I wasn't paying attention to during that time was that I was still a very negative person. Even though my self-talk was still highly disparaging and I was still abusing alcohol, I pulled portions of my life together, like getting myself out of debt and rebuilding my credit.

A couple of years after divorce, I met someone, fell in love, and got married. It wasn't long into this marriage that I came off the antidepressant, as instructed by my doctor. This new relationship was emotionally charged in ways both good and bad. It wasn't long after coming off the antidepressant that I did in fact relapse. Since we tended to fight, the depression was exacerbated by feelings of anger and resentment. In addition, there was rarely a period of stability at work with layoffs occurring once or twice a year. The new story I told myself was - this is what I deserve. I started to withdraw and detach emotionally in this relationship much like the last.

The shame was even stronger with a second depression. I felt like a failure as a human. People get up every day and are simply happy and they do this without the aid of medication, but I couldn't just be happy like a normal person. I had to start taking Prozac again and find a new therapist, but I repeated the cycle. The medication did its job and I didn't. I kept my true feelings in and only talked about issues I felt comfortable with. I focused on issues within the dynamic of the relationship. I was deflecting so I wouldn't have to address myself and my contribution to those issues. When it came to taking a real look at myself and delving into how I felt about myself, I wouldn't acknowledge what was mine to own. I was overwhelmed by feelings of shame. The shame comes from feeling inadequate or like I was never good enough or that I was totally worthless. The shame of not treating myself with kindness and compassion. The shame that comes from not feeling like a normal happy person, a person who felt he was failing to function as a human on such a basic level that he needed to be treated for depression, again.

Once again, I was taking Prozac, but still wasn't doing anything to address my feelings of shame and self-loathing. I felt embarrassed that I needed an antidepressant to feel better, so I stopped. I told myself I would never take it again because I was determined to make myself happy without it. It didn't go well. My wife and I separated a couple of times, but the last time finally led me to bottom out. It was June 2020, there were a lot of stressors at the time. We had an epic blowout and I left. That decision was taken out of my hands although I played a key role in having to leave. I started seeing a new therapist in July and was initially very angry during my sessions. In mid-August, we started talking about my struggles with depression and realized that I had been carrying around a lot of low-level hostility, and anger. Even my sense of humor had become self-deprecating and sarcastic, rooted in low self-esteem. Looking back on the last two decades of my life, it became clear I needed to change. I couldn't continue feeling miserable and angry at the world and myself. During a session, I said to her, "I'm tired of being angry all the time." I had labeled myself as "not good enough," unworthy and undeserving of happiness, what my therapist called a self-applied "Scarlet Letter." With her help I finally began to do the work, which required me to speak openly about how depression had shamed me into believing that I had no value.

Over the past year, with the help of my therapist, I began to explore the idea that unfulfilled dreams of being a professional artist were what caused my initial depression and what conditioned me to treat myself in a very unkind and disrespectful way. This conditioning would shape how I saw myself and would last for decades. I thought that her theory seemed a little dramatic. Like not pursuing that career path couldn't have been significant enough to cause depression. However, her theory was less about giving up on a career and more about giving up on myself. I came to realize that the episodes of depression I've experienced were the product of something bigger than not pursuing a career or unfulfilling jobs. By letting go of the dreams I had for my professional life I completely abandoned myself. I didn't just give up on a career, I gave up on who I am at my core. I denied my own needs and lost who I was on a fundamental level.

Through our work together, I began to embrace my experience and talk honestly. During one session, she asked me, "when was the last time you felt truly happy?" I had to think about this. Finally, I said, "I can remember feeling happy when I was a kid lying on my bedroom floor drawing". Then I corrected myself and talked to her about how wonderful I felt just a couple of years back when I started attending a Saturday morning Zazen meditation service. I stopped going to those services even though I felt great after each one. I had, once again, abandoned something that brought joy to my life. She encouraged me to start up a Zen meditation practice, which I did in October 2020.

At about the same time, I stopped abusing alcohol. I started creating art, on my terms, for the pleasure of it. By January 2021, a daily practice of meditation and mindfulness allowed me to accept myself just as I am, and I discovered for the first time, a true sense of peace within me. This consistent practice allowed me to see that I am worthy and have inherent value. This practice also reconditioned how I think and feel about myself, silencing my inner critic and negative self-talk. It brought a grounded presence to my life and relationships.

> "Authenticity demands Wholehearted living and loving – even when it's hard, even when we're wrestling with the shame and fear of not being good enough, and especially when the joy is so intense that we're afraid to let ourselves feel it.
>
> Mindfully practicing authenticity during our most soul-searching struggles is how we invite grace, joy, and gratitude into our lives."
>
> The Gifts of Imperfection, Brené Brown

I completely leaned into vulnerability, as unpleasant as it was to do at first. I opened up about things that caused me to feel ashamed in the past. Letting people it has allowed me to reconnect with friends, and I've cultivated new relationships that are so much more meaningful than before. In allowing my authentic self to be seen I believe I have been able to create a sense of safety for the people in my life to share their authentic selves.

I now lead my life with kindness, compassion, and empathy, letting go of anger and resentment. The universe continues to return to me the energy I put out to it, this time in a positive way. We all have our struggles - no one is perfect, but we are all enough. Treat yourself with kindness and don't fear who you are. There's liberation in living authentically.

ABOUT THE AUTHOR

ERIK SYMES

Erik Symes is an amateur artist, photographer, and the founder of his own life experience. He earned a Bachelor of Fine Arts from Southeastern Massachusetts University (now UMass Dartmouth) in 1991. He has worked the past 10 years for an educational publisher holding various roles within digital content management and archiving as well as platform implementation and development of an internal content management system with responsibilities focused on the user experience.

Erik is a creative who understands the therapeutic power of the arts. He is also a firm believer in the mental health benefits that can be realized through a consistent Zazen meditation and mindfulness practice. Through his story, he hopes to help alleviate the shame associated with depression. Erik currently resides in central Massachusetts, where he attempts, to the best of his abilities, to bring kindness, compassion, understanding, and empathy into a world that needs it more now than ever.

Instagram: https://www.instagram.com/grounded.evolving.man/

9
GRAHAM G WHEATCROFT

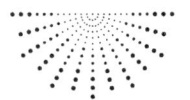

FROM ANXIETY TO A RESILIENT LIFESTYLE

You know those moments when you feel unfulfilled by what you're doing day to day, both personally and professionally.

Have you ever felt like this? I know I have. But that was the "old" me, a version of me that no longer served me well.

I'm here to share my journey about how I created this transformation for myself and to inspire you to discover your own resilience to keep moving forwards - even though the odds might seem stacked against you. This is more relevant today than ever before.

I'm a Remote Resilient Coach, helping people to live with less anxiety, achieve greater fitness, and keep a stronger connection with themselves. I'm also a married family man with two amazing kids and a very supportive family whom I love dearly.

THE PROBLEM

I was facing the challenges of a relationship breakdown, resulting in divorce. This was draining me physically, mentally, energetically, and spiritually. Looking back, I spent too much time and energy complicating life. Everything was draining my power, and my stress and anxiety levels were going through the roof.

At the time, my work was stressful, full of unrealistic expectations and insane working hours. I received little gratitude for the time and effort I put in. The daily grind was literally grinding me down.

I realised deep down that my relationship also wasn't working and that I no longer felt connected. I became a "people pleaser". I was happy to let others call the shots. I did little on my own terms, so my wishes never came first. There was no balance.

My spiritual practices of meditation and crystal healing disappeared entirely. I had become deprived of those important outlets that were keeping my mind calm and clear. I had conformed to the demands of other people in my life. I had allowed myself to be undermined, and I was no longer my authentic self.

Physically I had lost muscle and strength and hit burnout. I was trying to run multiple fitness classes alongside my day job and then show up as a family man. I had become a shadow of who I really wanted to be. It was chaotic. I was experiencing boredom, stress, fatigue, and a lack of interest in my job. I wanted out. I wanted to scream: "This is not who I am!!!" I had always wanted to create my own fitness and well-being business but had no idea how to make this a reality.

The whole experience of an unfulfilling job, a failing relationship, and a lack of spiritual connection all led to a severe breakdown.

I became very insular and felt that everyone was judging me. I often curled up on my bed, feeling paralysed by fear. I suffered three bouts of shingles in a short space of time, and my thoughts even became suicidal. At my mother's insistence, I visited my General Practitioner, only to be prescribed a powerful drug to deal with my severe anxiety —"if I needed it."

At this point, I needed to make a decision.

THE TURNING POINT

As a spiritual Aquarius, believing in a holistic approach, I became determined not to "fix" myself with medication. I quickly realised the need to return to the basics that I knew—the natural way.

Dragan lifting (exercising with dumbbells using the method created by Fitness4x4®), taking walks in nature, and returning to meditation —these became my "medicine".

It was about learning how to be comfortable in my own space and enjoy moments of solitude to focus on developing new and profound ways to restore balance in my life. I had to unlearn what had become expected of me by society itself and some of those around me. I even created my own "fortress of solitude" in the woods where I used to play as a kid. As a superhero fan, I often looked at Batman's journey, and the words of Alfred Pennyworth:

"Why do we fall? So we can learn to pick ourselves up".

The Dragan lifting became my key focus. I'm grateful to Dragan Radovic and his son Rajko, who taught me this method of training. The lifts are a physical meditation for me. I'd like to introduce this method of training to you. It only takes 10-15 minutes to complete initially:

1. Stand comfortably with your feet shoulder-width apart. Hold a dumbbell in each hand with the weight in front of your thigh.

2. With one arm, lift the dumbbell towards your shoulder by bending the elbow as if holding a hammer. Then lift it onto your shoulder before lifting it vertically without locking out your elbow. Natural movement is key.

3. Bend your arm and bring the weight back to your shoulder. Then extend your arm, lowering the weight to the thigh. Repeat with the other arm. You may find you naturally have a slight forward or sideways lean as you move the weight and engage the core. This is fine, but it should not hurt the back in any way.

4. As one weight goes above your head, the core muscles on the opposite side of your body will engage, helping you raise the dumbbell upwards. I would encourage deep controlled breathing on each repetition. Your heart rate will increase steadily as you repeat the lifts, so you get the added benefit of cardio, as well as a strength and endurance workout, maximising your results in a short space of time.

5. You can also vary the speed of the lifts. It should be calm and flowing, but still challenging. If you require something more meditative, you can close your eyes. This will enable you to feel the movement through your body. Take the action slowly so you really have an awareness of the movement right through to your fingertips.

6. If you don't have dumbbells, bottles of water will suffice.

THE SHIFT

Eventually, I made the bold decision to move away from my day job to focus on creating my dream to become a fitness entrepreneur. I was going to live life on my terms. My wife at the time thought I was crazy. I'll never forget her words:

"You'll never make it through your first month!"

The rabbit hole of divorce was accelerated. The divorce process took its toll, but in a strange way, the universe had sent me a gift - the opportunity to step into my authentic self and regain my power.

My self-employed fitness journey began when I started working as a personal trainer for a hotel chain. As a rookie, I trusted those around me to guide me as I improved my coaching skills. However, this was not the case. I identified areas that seemed at odds with what I expected. My "manager" was a man of only words but no real action, and this resulted in an increasing amount of frustration for me. I decided to make the break.

THE PATHWAY

I had built up a stronghold of very loyal clients. So, when I chose to leave the hotel to set up elsewhere, they all came with me. Over time I discovered my new business and I were on a journey of growth together as we continued to discover our own authentic identities.

As I was reinventing myself and searching for the right business name, I used personal journaling, visualisation, and deep meditation. The word *"resilient"* kept appearing, and even the logo that would represent my new branding - **The Resilient Lifestyle**. With this discovery, I had realised my personal journey from anxiety to resilience. In my darkest hours I could have never have envisaged this pathway, but I also knew that I could help others who might be on a similar journey to find their own resilience and inner strength.

THE NEW PARADIGM

As the Covid pandemic struck and life generally moved to a remote and online learning paradigm, so my thinking became clearer. I moved my business away from rented premises to a home base. This seemed a natural transition. I converted my garage into a new home studio. It has become a very personal but also practical space, with a great vibe after receiving the joy of Feng Shui

Having the confidence to do this was the best decision I ever made. The space is truly my own. It still needs some work, but it is somewhere I can be myself, by myself, and also create a great experience for clients from anywhere in the world.

This is where I am right now on my journey.

INSPIRATIONS

In 2018 I attended an event in San Diego called "Warrior Con", led by Garrett J. White as part of his Wake Up Warrior movement. It was aimed at getting family and business men to raise their game across all areas of life. I learnt strategies and mindsets for which I am truly grateful, and still execute to this day. These have been a big influence on how I show up as a creator, a father, a husband, and a businessman. The process has also has seen a huge change in how I commit to my body and mind welfare, balance in my family life, and acceleration in my business.

Warrior was where I met one of my international clients, Alan, from New England, USA. He has had an amazing personal journey whilst training with me, and he has continued to train with me for some three years on. It's become a lifestyle change for him. He has achieved massive results, and his diabetes is under control. Here's what he has to say:

> *"I knew I needed help and accountability to get me to be prepared. When Graham reached out to me that day, it felt like forces were trying to help me. We did an honest "Where are you at today?" assessment and "Where do you want to go?" exercise, which truthfully exposed the damage I had done to myself over the years. But that was OK. It was exactly what I needed. Graham and I began working together a couple of days a week, and I began to feel stronger. Challenging myself to create and incorporate fitness into my lifestyle has been the most rewarding experience.*
>
> *"Also, having a Coach who knows what you are going through, and helps you understand the program and new lifestyle and habits you are building to become the best version of yourself, is huge. Graham and I continue to work towards my future goals. My body health and path to "weaponisation" is the driver for everything in my life. It funnels down into my life balance, being an example for my kids and my business, giving me the energy and passion every day.*

> "Graham continues to help me play the game of fitness week after week. You can't do it alone. Today I am down 75 lbs on my way to 125 lbs and the new Alan."

Alan has since reached his target of losing 125 lbs and then some more. He also completed a SAS style training course, survived a quadruple heart bypass, and is growing his own business.

Another client, Rachy from West Yorkshire, UK, has had an amazing journey since she began training with me. She is a particularly big fan of the Dragan lifts, and has overcome many challenges, creating huge change for herself:

> "I am writing this testimonial as I don't think I could record it without becoming an emotional wreck.
>
> "I have worked with Graham for eight months now. In that time I have overcome hurdles but equally found myself facing bigger hurdles. Each time, we (Graham and I together) have broken the hurdles down to make them easier to jump over.
>
> "I completed the 12-week Acceleration Program, it was truly a fantastic experience. It helped me take training to the next level. I increased my training time, took on so much information from Graham. I had essential oils delivered, and enjoyed a wellness workshop with his wife Lisa, as well as experiencing meditation techniques with Graham. Altogether, these things increased my physical and mental attitudes, and also helped me say goodbye to some demons.
>
> "Within the twelve weeks, my hip deteriorated, and so we had to focus on upper body. When the deterioration was evident, and I saw my GP, he was gobsmacked and very confused as to how I could actually walk with my hip in such a bad state. He told me to keep doing what I was doing because, even though using crutches, I was

defying medical science. In my mind Graham did this. He helped me by working on the key muscle groups around my hip, and we have managed to strengthen my hip enough to keep me mobile. I will be eternally grateful. Not only is Graham an amazing trainer, he is now a valued friend too."

Rachy has now committed herself and upgraded to the One Year Acceleration Program. She is continuing to make great progress, having personal revelations and discovering a whole new outlook on life.

Alan and Rachy are just a couple of inspirational individuals within The Resilient Lifestyle community, affectionately known as "The Wolfpack".

One of my biggest wins has been having the opportunity to help so many individuals—physically, mentally and spiritually—generally aged between 40 and 70. My oldest clients are about to reach 78. Friendships have been born as clients have got to know each other, and it makes me feel immensely proud to see how mutually supportive everybody is. I also appreciate how much they value the gifts my wife and I teach them, and the level of trust and respect we all have for one another.

THE GOOD THINGS HAPPEN IN THE PAUSES

When I reflect back to the beginning of my story, and how far I have come, I know the "new" version of me is a completely unrecognisable, expanded, and a changed version of who I had become. Discovering how to create a resilient lifestyle that is true to me, across my fitness, mindset, family life, and professionally, has been a profound experience. The beauty has been finding the simplicity in the process and keeping it time-efficient and manageable around daily life.

Change is good, and as my wonderful wife Lisa would say:

"The good things happen in the pauses".

The pathway doesn't just stop though. It continues each and every day. Small actions create the big wins. You just need a strategy and process with which you can remain consistent. This is why I love coaching people, helping them to accelerate their journeys, by teaching them what I have learned myself as a result of my own struggles, giving them the courage and belief to change and move forward.

The freedom you experience when you truly begin to find yourself is liberating. It creates confidence in the way you walk, talk, and even the way you dress. I firmly believe that the universe sends us these life "interrupts" to guide us to where we are supposed to be. The road may not be an easy one, or even seem clear, but one way or another it often makes sense in the end.

By choosing to take action consistently you begin the process of growth and change, physically, mentally, and spiritually. You will become resilient. It can seem daunting at first but it's never too late to start. The time investment to action the steps towards achievement is small. But with a little commitment, not just motivation, you can get there.

If you feel that my story inspires you, and that I can help you learn more about how to live **The Resilient Lifestyle**, I invite you to reach out through my social media links.

As I leave you today, I offer you this gift - my own little daily mantra:

"I choose to feel ease, to breathe, to flow and to grow. I am resilient."

Or, just say the words when your spirits would like a lift. To deepen the experience, sit comfortably and breathe through the nose whilst saying each word. Inhale for a count of four, then hold for four, exhale for four, and hold for four - and then repeat. Be present with the words, and your breath. Enjoy.

Ease.

Breathe.

Flow.

Grow.

And finally, to complete the experience say: *"I am resilient".*

Acknowledgments:
Thank you to Jenny, a true "Rainbow Warrior" and dear friend, for helping me bring this chapter to life.

ABOUT THE AUTHOR
GRAHAM G WHEATCROFT

Graham G Wheatcroft, fitness and resilience coach, faced anxiety issues that led him to feel in a dark place and a very low point in his life. He was determined to break free from this downward spiral.

Graham began daily deep work into physical, mental, and spiritual meditation, which have now become habits and commitments that he teaches his clients to help them build their own fitness and resilience and practices himself, using simple tools such as dumbbells and Breathwork.

Graham now delivers his remote time efficient coaching globally, is an Executive Contributor for Brainz Magazine, has been published digitally for Networking Magazine, the Medic Alert Foundation, and he has his own podcast: "The Resilient Lifestyle Podcast".

Social Media Links:
Facebook: www.facebook.com/resilientmanleader
Instagram: www.instagram.com/theresilientlifestyle?r=nametag
LinkedIn: www.linkedin.com/in/graham-g-wheatcroft-61476952

10
GREG SPECTOR

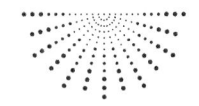

MY KINTSUKUROI SOUL

Scratch flicker sulfur floating across the fuse

Stick of dynamite packaged tight

Coiled in fear of ember and spark

Alive in the dark retreated from light

Chaos violence inevitable rage

Fierce noise light heat

Diminishing glow

And in the wake of destruction

.....Silence grows

"I'm an alcoholic." Admitting it is half the battle, right? BULLSHIT! It was only the first lonely step of a lengthy venture. A scary, humiliating, torturous sentence. Eclipsing anything I've ever admitted before. AND, it doesn't have a close second. So, half the battle—Hardly. How did I get from that admission to here? Lots and lots of hard fucking work! People in my corner who wouldn't quit on me or let me off the hook. Several trips to the hospital. Several stays in treatment centers (yes plural). Multiple rehabs (again plural, sensing a theme here?). Long days of self-discovery painted in the gloss of therapy, both inpatient and outpatient, fortunately with innumerable people who saw something I couldn't at the time—HOPE.

My ego stands sentry over all my characteristics and qualities that humanity would consider positive attributes to society at large. I therefore cannot truly be introspective and at minimum seek my authentic self without cutting a deal with the gatekeeper of my soul. As I proceed in my search and continue to discover my basic emotions, fears, gratitude, and pride I am consistently sidestepping the chaos and myre of my ego, who appears endlessly armed and seemingly impossible.

When I first considered writing my story on the topic of the Authentic self, the process felt crushing and daunting. I would need to discover how I got here. I wasn't even sure I knew what or where here even was. This is Addiction with a capital A. No one signs up for addiction. Last I checked, being an alcoholic wasn't a career goal. Even if it was, who would choose it?

The path to my authentic self has been a meandering and arduous one. Layered and filled with the challenges of character and spiritual deficits, emotional stagnation, fear, self-loathing, sadness, anger, pity, and their leader-MY EGO. While all of us have an ego and it is a necessary component of a healthy well-adjusted person, mine tends to run amok when unchecked. My ego stands before my gratitude, faith, and spirituality employing fear, anger, sadness, resentments; its goal is deterring me from my authentic self. Regaining my self would become a years-long street fight with the largest trophy going to the winner. The sharp iron odor of blood would spill forth and settle upon me like a weighted blanket, oddly comforting in its familiarity.

My illness grew within me quietly, unbeknownst to me until late in my drinking career. I always "got away with it". Whatever "it" was. I either knowingly or unconsciously aligned myself with those who would normalize my drinking. As a young teen, I drank and "partied" with my friends (The Heads). We were "those guys"—the cool ones everyone wanted at their parties. This arena was where I began to use alcohol to diminish or hide my self-perceived deficiencies. The masses thought I belonged to the cool crowd and I would be damned if they discovered the truth. It was then that I started to build the foundation of the larger than life Greg. I made sure that no one knew or saw the insecure, scared, confused, uncomfortable me. I began to perfect my external character and he slowly began to function as the person everyone else came to know. I had to...NEEDED to...be over the top and prove seemingly on a daily basis that I was the craziest of the bunch.

Driving The Heads to a party during the summer of 1987 I was already on my way to being drunk, having started earlier than everyone else to ensure that my shields were firmly in place and that my alter ego had ample time to rise from the shadows and assume his place at the forefront. During the drive out to the valley, a young girl of only ten years old stuck her tongue at me from the back seat of her family station wagon. There was no way in hell this little shit was going to get the better of me! I told my friend in the passenger seat to take the wheel and the gas pedal, which meant he was now driving the van from the passenger's seat on the highway in LA traffic. I proceeded to drop my shorts and hang my naked ass out the driver's side window at this little girl. I laughed and laughed as well as did the collective drunks in the van. Who does that shit? I had achieved my goal of being the craziest one of the day. In hindsight, I view it as one of many many poor decisions I made along my journey. But, I got away with it. That recurring theme would follow me and eventually be the detriment of my physical, emotional and spiritual self. I would lose nearly everything important to me. No, not yet, not by a long shot. I still had sports, college, a professional career, and two marriages to completely soak in booze before I was through.

The lofty height and width of the pedestal we place sports and the athletes who participate in them on in our society is ridiculous. We all have heard the stories of the jock who "got away with it". Need a grade raised? Need a ticket or complaint to disappear? Didn't behave in a socially responsible manner? No worries, we got it covered. That was my world. As a young man who peddled in lies and mirrors, I ate it up. My high school basketball coach/trigonometry teacher gave me a "D" in math when I most assuredly deserved an "F" because to do otherwise would have made me ineligible to play hoops. Just a small sample of life as an athlete.

OGRE! My alter ego now had a name. When I pledged a fraternity in college and was officially bestowed the title I thought "damn straight, now I can really get busy building my castle of beer cans and bottles where my ego would stand upon the altar and be lavished with the praise he so desired and needed". Every day was an opportunity to display my prowess at the top of the alcoholic food chain. I found my way to a position as the Sergeant at Arms that supplied Ogre with the adoration and respect he felt he deserved. I was the man at the door of all our parties. Everyone had to pass me to get in. The power and respect that came with that title were everything I desired and needed.

Coaching was a natural progression from my athletic self into an abyss of continued drinking. The profession is riddled with examples of former and current alcoholics who surround themselves with like-minded individuals who seek victory at all costs and utilize maximum effort to arrive there. On my journey through coaching, I easily met as many coaches who had a bottle of liquor in their desk drawer as those who didn't. See if you can guess which of the two categories I poured into?

Using the lessons I learned from the lunacy that was my first marriage I was determined to never repeat the missteps of my past in my second. True to my word, I didn't. Instead, I found new and fantastic ways to demolish my second marriage. Having lost all space and time in the bottle, my tolerance for anything that hindered the daily infusion of what I perceived as a necessary component of life, I shunned and pushed away everyone who would have helped save me from the impending misery I was rocketing towards. My dissolution of the grandiose ego I had developed was as unhealthy to my family relationships as if I became physically violent. I adapted the mentality that all bad things were happening to me and not because of me. After several years on the roller coaster with multiple derailments from the highest peaks of success crashing to the deepest valleys of despair my family was through. I was no longer able to sustain both a drinking career and my family...I had not chosen wisely. I found new and increasingly crippling ways to generate self-loathing and pity where none was merited and set ablaze a demonic fire launching feckless platitudes on the path before me as I walked away from the family I had once held so dear.

As I mentally reconcile my marriages, there is that ugly plural again, I realize that alcohol distorted my proximity to the truth so deftly that I could not see the trainwreck of a movie that I was the lead character in. The two trains of marriage that I had conducted found their way into colliding. Sharing their truths, I cannot drive my own will. My train always ran the fastest and hit the hardest. Leaving a vacuum of lives to deal with the wreckage where I was no longer present to acknowledge nor assist in the restoration.

Close your eyes and think back to the most painful event of your life. Now, think about a time you were so terrified you couldn't scream. What's the saddest moment of your life? When did you feel completely helpless? Can you remember being so angry you could kill? How about so much misery you wished you would just die already? Bring all of that into one thought, one steady stream of existence, and relive it every day. Now you're an alcoholic who might...MIGHT be ready to seek a new way of living. Daily life for me in rehab was devastatingly painful and the concert played over and over in my body, mind, and spirit. My body was as close to losing its battle with life as I care to ever think about. For years I lived life outside of time. I had no connections to reality other than the crippling illness that I subjected my body to every second, minute, and hour of every day. The only way out, the only way back to normal was through the scorching 5-alarm fire setting ablaze to my ego and bringing it down to ashes. In December I lay crying in the fetal position in rehab, losing and regaining my mind in a never-ending oscillation of fear and shame, feeling my heart pounding like a massive rotor on a helicopter trapped in my chest, and doing what my flesh and muscles and will seemed incapable of achieving. Sustaining my life one shattering slam against my chest wall at a time like a sledgehammer convinced if it struck the anvil hard enough it would split and provide me with freedom.

My shadow side and I have a special relationship—like a mistress from my past who falls into step with me when I am not paying attention. Begging me to join in the sexy fun and who-gives-a-shit antics we used to share, daring me to come back to the cool soft illusion provided by the shadow of drinking. The alluring dance we share momentarily masks the chaos and darkness that hides there in the soft light of the shadow. Try to shine a light on this darkness all you wish, it deftly glides like a well-trained ballerina away from the exposure and truth the light would bring. My shadow uses me to protect it from the truth. I am the guardian - only I can expose our secrets, reveal the scars, blemishes, games, and actions we shared. But how will the protective nature of my ego react, as it was built to keep my ugliness in the shadows so no one would see them? What would happen if I dared expose them or god forbid, learned to live with them.

Today I give myself permission to be sober in the way I used to give myself permission to drink. Each day I found a reason to drink, a reason to say fuck it. Every day was a different solution with the same ending of a pitiful, soulless story of mental weakness and regret. Today, with my permission and persuasion I allow myself to be sober. I allow myself to feel, cry, laugh, hug, and hold myself without the need to activate my inhibitions to do so. Alcohol sits next to me sometimes and we talk, like old friends with a troubled and wary past. My shadow looks at those times in a much fonder light than I do. But, we can talk about it now and I forgive alcohol as I hope alcohol will forgive me. Since I am inescapably tethered to my shadow, who acts as an anchor creating an eddy that returns my life to the whirlpool of regret and destruction, I found I need to consciously choose to put my shadow where it belongs—BEHIND ME. So I can face the sun and look towards the warmth, joy, and endless possibilities provided in the light. My shadow will have to join me and go along for the journey as we are forever attached. However, the role I allow my shadow to play in my life today is a choice that resides solely within me.

My mind is a confusing concert of ideas that collide, light up, glow fade and send a clatter and shattering din across the screen of my mind's thoughts. Think of it as a pinball machine with 1000 shining pinballs flying undeterred until they collide and generate noise, light, piercing my train of thought. I get confused, angry, and disappointed. Why can't I focus and get shit done? Remember telling your wife you'd "take care of it?" Of course, you don't! So my solution was to take a massive brick of alcohol and heave it at the machine with every ounce of energy I could muster. Destroying all chains of thought. Now broken and in disarray with the steel silver flashy ideas rolling away to find a dark corner in the shadows of my mind to fade away. No longer bringing attention to themselves. Leaving me alone with my thoughts, with nothing.

While sitting at reverend Todd's altar in the chair of his tattoo parlor shuffling my feet through the dust of my mind and the story I need to tell but am terrified to write, Todd shared some of his great wisdom with me. He reminded me that lessons enter the path of our lives seemingly at random, the when and how they join us is an enormous part of finding, acknowledging, and revealing our authentic selves to the world. Once my truth is spoken it no longer belongs to me. It is now part of the collective conscience. It doesn't change but it does grow, strengthen, and gain clarity when exposed to the interpretations of others. And therefore becomes part of their story and journey as well. Ideally, my truth will help someone to begin to realize their authenticity and all that they have to offer. In this, I have found one crowning achievement...My own HUMAN IMPERFECTION.

Knowing your authentic self doesn't heal the shattered vessel you once were, but it does allow you to work on the puzzle of rebuilding your future self. As occurs in kintsukuroi, the Japanese art of repairing broken pottery by mending the areas of breakage with lacquer dusted or mixed with powdered gold, silver, or platinum. As a philosophy, it treats breakage and repair as part of the beauty and history of an object, rather than something to disguise.

My Kintsukuroi Soul
Once broken strewn spinning across the landscape
Desperately collecting the pieces
Gripping them securing them tightly they pierce the space
Fingers dripping with crimson essence
Cracked marred beauty within the scars told new and old

Pieces joining veins of gold melting filling the void
Pulling together old stories and memories a resemblance to new
Gold pictured veins of blood supplying hope beauty and joy
Aglow with new life infusing
Not hiding, not running. Flowing joining in a new marriage
...Spirited. Forward. Dancing.

ABOUT THE AUTHOR

GREG SPECTOR

Greg Spector is an educator, coach, and writer. Born in Encino, CA, Greg holds a B.S. in Applied Kinesiology from SDSU and an M.Ed. from Urbana University, Ohio. The son of an accountant and teacher who adopted him at a wee seven days old. They had no idea the highest mountains and deepest valleys that would accompany Greg home with them.

Greg played competitive level volleyball, basketball, soccer, and team handball, and started coaching volleyball at age 19. In his chapter, Greg allows the reader a glimpse inside the athlete's winning mindset. He reveals what happens when that same mindset is applied to other areas of his life, specifically alcohol. He guides the reader through a raw, uninhibited look inside the fight with the greatest opponent of his lifetime--Alcohol. There he finally discovers that winning means losing it all.

In his spare time, Greg enjoys spending time with his family, reading, writing, and fishing.

Website: www.twenty4more.com
Instagram: www.instagram.com/twenty.4.more/
Facebook: www.facebook.com/groups/410550124060302
Linked In: www.linkedin.com/in/greg-spector-b060b323/
Email: twenty4more.spector@gmail.com

11

JULIE MAIGRET SHAPIRO

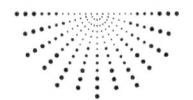

AWAKENING TO MY DREAMS

"Tell me, what is it you plan to do with your one wild and precious life?" - Mary Oliver

---

I was desperate for change and tired of living life on the sidelines. My dreams had taken a backseat to the all-consuming obligations of caregiving for my ailing mother and a demanding job. I expected more from my life, yet my dreams were buried so deep inside that they seemed out-of-reach. I felt numb and out of touch with my desires.

Things started to shift during an off-site work retreat. At the time, I was working at UC Berkeley in a department dedicated to leadership programs for professionals. Our Dean was young, brilliant, ambitious, and open-minded. She encouraged us to grow as leaders by consistently pushing us out of our comfort zones. At our monthly team off-sites, she had us try out the hottest trends in leadership development and team-building. We dabbled in many kinds of experiential learning exercises, including equine-assisted leadership and empathy training, team-building through rowing, trust exercises, improv and theatrical techniques for effective communication.

At first, I completely dreaded the off-site days. They were intense, and left me feeling exposed and vulnerable.Eventually, I started to appreciate these learning experiences. I realized how fortunate I was to have the opportunity to develop myself in my workplace. Some of the retreats focused on personality assessments to help us understand and maximize our unique strengths within the context of the team. As a lifelong self-help junkie, these were the ones I liked best.

On this particular day, our Dean had brought in an expert on the Enneagram. I did not know the Enneagram and was thrilled to learn a new way to understand my personality type. The facilitator started the day with an icebreaker to warm us up. Afterwards, we took a quick assessment to determine our enneagram type.

Initially excited, my mood turned to panic and dread once I saw my results.

My type was 2: The Helper.

The Enneagram Institute says that Helpers (also known as the Givers): "are empathetic, sincere, and warm-hearted. They are friendly, generous, and self-sacrificing, but can also be sentimental, flattering, and people-pleasing."

There are very positive things about my Enneagram type that I identify with: being generous, kind, and wanting to help others. However, the description of their "shadow side" made me pause: They can be self-sacrificing, people-pleasing, manipulative, and co-dependent.

Reading my Enneagram results was like having someone hold up a mirror up and show me things I hadn't wanted to see about myself. I knew that I had codependent tendencies, but it wasn't until then that I realized how much this was holding me back in my life.

Ashamed of my results, I felt my stomach tense and sank down in my chair. I tried to hide my paper, feeling disgusted at myself. This revelation hit a nerve because it was a theme that kept coming up in my life at that time.

Ever since I started working at the business school, I noticed that people were criticizing me for the very traits that I thought were my best qualities.

Several people at work told me I was "too nice." At first I thought it was a compliment, but soon enough, I realized they meant I did not have good boundaries. In their minds, I was letting people take advantage of me, and they didn't respect me for that.

It was difficult for me to reconcile that what I considered my strongest asset was perceived as a weakness.

Looking back at my childhood, it makes sense that I didn't have an understanding of healthy boundaries. When I was seven years old, my parents threw a big party with their younger hippie friends. They loved to entertain and were known for their generosity and extravagance. I remember that it was late on a school night. Lying in my bed, I couldn't sleep because the music from below my bedroom was so loud. I came out of my room and looked down onto the living room from our mezzanine. My parents and their friends were dancing wildly to "Light My Fire" by the Doors. Feeling upset and helpless, I didn't know what to do. No one noticed as I watched them from upstairs.

After contemplating my options, I couldn't take it anymore. Knowing I had to go to school the next day emboldened me to say something. I raised my voice as loud as I could and asked them to please turn the music down. Everyone looked up at me, surprised. My parents were embarrassed and sheepishly turned the music way down. The party wound down soon after. Relieved, I returned to my bedroom. That night in bed, I pondered what had just happened. Quietly delighting in my win, it was also awkward and confusing. I was supposed to be the child here!

My parents had big personalities and could be overbearing and volatile. I knew they loved me, but their erratic parenting style didn't allow me to simply be a child. Both were emotional in their own way. They fought frequently, forcing me into the role of peacekeeper and harmonizer.

My father was a psychologist with a successful private practice. He was bright, handsome, and charming to the world, but could be emotionally distant and irritable at home. When I was young, he worked long hours and often returned home in a bad mood.

Brilliant, beautiful and sexy, my mother was a catch. When they first met, my father was smitten and determined to win her heart. However, once they were married, my father's compulsive womanizing crushed her spirit and she soon lost her footing in the relationship. They eventually divorced. Abandoned by my father and depressed, my mother compensated for her loss by relying on me for emotional support. I was her only child, and she centered her world around me. She was warm, generous, and indulgent, but also extremely vulnerable and needy.

Within our family dynamic, there wasn't much room for my needs, wants, and emotions—so I kept them to myself. I had to take on an adult role early on and learned to be self-reliant and independent.

The behaviours I learned in childhood continued to play out throughout my life.

Tending to others' needs above my own became a pattern. My reputation as kind, generous, and trustworthy made it easy for me to make friends and attract romantic partners. However, my lack of boundaries created a lot of grief and disappointment in my relationships. It was difficult for me to set limits and speak up for myself to ensure my needs were met. I was keenly aware that something was out of balance—but I didn't know how to fix it.

At work, however, my self-sacrificing behavior was often rewarded. My tendency to be overly accommodating made me a perfect fit for my job at the time in program management. I worked around the clock: on weekends, evenings, and holidays. My job entailed taking care of large groups of participants attending our programs. I was responsible for planning and coordinating every detail for each of my programs with the professors, clients, and other stakeholders.

I was the person in charge, the producer who put together all the details for complex multi-day programs with groups from around the world. And that felt good! There were endless details to manage, and we worked long hours to make sure that everything ran smoothly. I received a lot of praise for my dedication, attention to detail, and "extraordinary" customer service. Knowing that I was making a positive impact kept me going.

Despite my success, I realized that my helper instinct was holding me back in my career. On the one hand, I was rewarded for my hard work and conscientiousness. On the other hand, I wasn't always respected by my co-workers. The faculty loved that their programs ran seamlessly. Nevertheless, in trying so hard to please everyone, I had given up my power and made myself less visible. I was always on and attentive to everyone's requests and had no time for myself. Perpetually exhausted, I saw the vicious cycle: the better I did at my job, the more invisible and less valued I felt.

Burned out, I recognized that this pattern wasn't healthy or sustainable. By making everyone's agenda more important than mine, I was hiding out and avoiding what really mattered to me.

Women still take on the majority of helper/caregiving roles in our society. Taking care of others is often all-consuming, leaving us worn out with little time for ourselves. We dream of a bigger life, but we don't have the time or space to nurture our dreams.

Our deep desires often reemerge in midlife when we become aware of our own mortality. This can be a powerful time of reawakening when we are called to explore our long neglected desires and goals. After years of putting our dreams on hold, they begin to take up space in our psyches and force us to reexamine our lives.

Being labeled a two on the Enneagram was an unpleasant wake-up call for me. Painfully aware that I wasn't living up to my potential, I felt like a failure.

All in all, my uncomfortable relevation was both a blessing and a reckoning. With time, I came to terms with my despair. I had been on the wrong path, and I did not want to go where it was leading me. Here was my opportunity to correct the course.

I understood that I would never get the respect I desired without better boundaries. I needed to stop over being overly accommodating and self-abandoning.

So I started to set boundaries. Respecting my limits, made a big difference in my energy level and boosted my confidence. I was no longer constantly exhausted from overgiving and overdoing. This gave me more space to think about my life and goals. It also widened my perspective, allowing me to see more options and make different choices.

It became clear that my current job was no longer healthy for me since it rewarded the self-sacrificing behaviors I was trying to avoid. Besides, I no longer enjoyed being mired in the details of program management. Focusing on so many time-critical tasks had overwhelmed me and narrowed my perspective. Instead, I needed to expand my vision of what was possible.

The fear of venturing out of my comfort zone started falling away as I gained the courage to pursue new goals. Ready to get out of my own way and embrace a bigger life, I began to ask for what I wanted. Most importantly, I started believing in myself.

For a long while, I had considered applying for a business development role on our team. I hadn't told anyone because I didn't have the experience and wasn't sure if I would be good at it. Deep down though, I knew that I could handle it and I was ready to take the risk. When there was an opening, I applied and got the job.

At first, I felt like I was fumbling in the dark in my new role. I didn't know what I was doing, and there was no training. Fortunately, building relationships was something that I was naturally good at and enjoyed. My role was to help clients solve their organizational challenges through educational programs. Designing customized learning experiences that transformed mindsets and skill sets gave me a deep sense of satisfaction. Communicating my vision was an important part of the process, and I no longer felt invisible.

Although I still worked hard, I found that in this role, there was more space for me to be my authentic self. My job required me to have a large-scale view. This helped me to see my work and my life through a wider lens. Witnessing the positive impact that our programs made on the participants and their organizations was gratifying and on target with our organizational mission.

Taking on this new role was rewarding both personally and professionally. I was happier, I had more control over my time, and was making more money. I even started to appreciate many of my Enneagram 2 qualities, including my talent for relationship building. I was excelling in my new role, and that gave me the courage to ask for a promotion.

With my newfound confidence, I ended up negotiating a new title, a substantial raise, and an office.

Looking back, it's remarkable that I could go from feeling completely powerless in my life to having a sense of agency. Understanding my unhealthy behaviors and patterns was key to transcending them and designing a better future.

Having experienced my own transformation, I realized that I wanted to help other women navigate the challenges and opportunities of midlife. I'm committed to championing women who feel stuck and uninspired and encouraging them to step up and make their mark in the world. My mission is to help women thrive in their careers, find work that nourishes their souls and gives them a sense of purpose.

So how do *you* move towards your dreams?

For those of you who are feeling stuck in your life, I have created a simple 4-step process to get you moving towards your dreams:

My process involves cultivating curiosity, self-compassion, creativity, courage, and connection.

Step 1: Reconnect with your joy and curiosity:

I invite you to begin your journey with a large dose of curiosity.

First make a list of:

- What brings you joy
- What you loved as a child
- Things you are grateful for
- What you are curious to learn about

Now it's time to visualize your ideal life:

Prepare yourself by finding a quiet and relaxing space where you won't be disturbed. You might put on soothing music or light candles to get in the mood. Then, sit in a comfortable position and take a few breaths. Next, close your eyes and start to visualize your desired future. Use these questions as prompts:

- What does your ideal life look like?
- What about this life makes you happy?
- What are you proud of?
- How do you feel?
- What or who are you grateful for?
- What are you doing?
- What are you known for?

Now, take notes reflecting on everything you have visualized.

Step 2. Reflect on your situation with Self-Compassion

This step involves delving deep into what you feel, what you want, what's working, and what's not working. The important part is to examine your life without judgement.

I encourage you to cultivate a "beginner's mind." This means having an attitude of openness and setting aside any preconceptions. Look at your life from an outside perspective. Honor yourself with self-compassion.

For step two, it is key to relax your mind. Before you begin, clear your schedule, find a calm space, and take some deep breaths. Then grab a journal or sketch pad and answer these questions:

- What does my dream of a bigger life look like? Be specific!
- Why is this important to me?
- How will it change my life?
- How do I want to feel?
- What would I need to change about myself?
- What scares me?
- Where am I stuck?
- What is holding me back?
- What do I need to let go of?
- What am I gaining from staying in my current situation?
- What is not working in my life now?
- What steps can I take to move forward?

If negative emotions or judgements arise, take a break and breathe into them.

Step 3. Experiment with Creativity and Courage

This step is about taking action and testing your ideas. Allow creativity to be your guide, and make this fun. Experiment with new ideas using this Design Thinking technique.

Phase I

- Take out your notes from your visioning session and read them over
- Once you have a clear vision of your dream, imagine what steps you'll need to take
- Try to be open to all ideas - even the ones that seem impossible
- Take 20-30 minutes to write down all your ideas
- Write each idea on a separate Post-it sticker
- Once you have written all of your ideas down, place them on a wall or surface
- Organize them into categories
- Pick your top 3

Phase II

Now, it is time to create an action plan and try out some of these ideas. Remember, these are meant to be mini-experiments—so adopt a playful mindset.

For example, if you are considering starting a podcast, you might plan out steps like these:

- Listen to your favorite podcast and take notes on what you liked
- Write out possible podcasts topics that interest you
- Connect with a podcaster to interview them about their process

I suggest that you break each action into micro-steps that are easy to accomplish. Make them as small and easy as possible!

Step 4: Leverage Your Connections and Extend Your Reach

Letting others help you can bolster your confidence and expand your network.

Some ideas:

- Ask for support from a friend or colleague
- Schedule an informational interview with someone doing what you want to do
- Expand your network by joining an association or attending a conference
- Brainstorm with a mentor, coach or friend

When you feel stuck or knocked down by life's trials and tribulations, remember this can be an opportunity to move forward in a new direction. Start small, but think big. The first thing to do is let go of beliefs and behaviors that no longer serve you. Experiment with different ways of showing up in the world. Your life is rich with possibilities — choose to make it a great one.

"When I let go of who I am, I become who I might be." - Lao Tzu

---

You're on your way. I wish you luck on your journey!

ABOUT THE AUTHOR
JULIE MAIGRET SHAPIRO

Julie is a women's career empowerment coach dedicated to enhancing opportunities for midlife women. She created 'Women Who Stay in the Game' to help women over 40 find their passion and purpose, share their unique gifts with the world, and flourish in their careers.

During her international career, she has worked in academia and industry. Most recently, Julie was a Learning and Development leader at UC Berkeley. She loves to travel and has lived in Italy, France, and Spain. Julie holds a BA from UC Berkeley and a Master's from Middlebury College. She is a certified coach from Berkeley Executive Coaching Institute.

In her chapter, Julie reveals how letting go of beliefs that no longer serve us can open us up to new possibilities.

Julie can be reached at:
Instagram: www.instagram.com/womenwhostayinthegame/
FB: www.facebook.com/womenwhostayinthegame
LinkedIn: www.linkedin.com/in/juliejmshapiro/
Website: WomenWhoStayintheGame.com

12

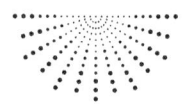

KAMIL SHAH

AN ARCHITECT'S GUIDE TO BUILDING AN AUTHENTIC LIFE

In the opening scene of 'Jim & Andy – The Great Beyond', Hollywood movie star, funnyman, and conscious being, Jim Carrey was asked "How would you start this movie?". Without hesitation, Jim, still shuffling in his chair, replied "Well, if I had my choice, it wouldn't start at all. It would already have been. And it wouldn't end either. You know, when *did* this movie start?".

When I was asked to write this chapter and share my story, I asked myself the same question.

"When did *my* movie start?"

Prior to becoming a Certified Life Coach, I was doing the 9-5 practicing Architecture while raising my beautiful family. Everything seemed to have its place. However, I felt that there was something still missing. Looking back, I saw myself just surviving from one day to the next. I have since found that what was missing was there all along inside of me and just needed to be switched 'ON'. It just needed deep reflection and observing my past from a different point of view.

In this chapter, I will share with you my journey through Architecture, a profession which was chosen for me growing up, but one which upon reflection has taught me some powerful life lessons along the way.

FOUNDATION - THE ART OF BELIEVING

In Architecture, the foundation of any building is fundamental. Without a proper understanding of the surrounding soil composition, applying a certain foundation design can either make or break the building. This is a great analogy when applying it to building an authentic life. Applying the right foundation strategy can make a solid and long-standing structure that lasts a lifetime. Applying the wrong approach to building your 'foundation' can spell D-I-S A-S-T-E-R.

This is where this chapter begins and that is with the foundations of 'belief'.

Although I was born in Malaysia, our family moved a lot when I was growing up. When I was about 5, we moved to Madison, Wisconsin. Not only was it my first trip abroad, it was my first ever move to a foreign land. It was daunting at first, but I enjoyed my younger life there. It proved to be one of the fondest memories I have of my childhood. Moving to far-off lands also meant that I had to say 'Hi' and 'Goodbye' to many people including friends and teachers.

Among all of the new people I had met growing up, there is one particular teacher whom, if I were to perchance meet again one day, I would give him a big hug and say "Thank You!". He had taught me a lesson that would later form one of my core character strengths. If fully understood, this powerful lesson containing just four words can profoundly change the way we live our lives by opening new doors, making new pathways, and creating new connections.

Here's the story.

When I was 13, I moved back to Malaysia and joined another new school. First lesson of my first day was Science. On hearing my name being called out, I raised my hand and said "Yes sir!" to acknowledge my attendance to the teacher.

Pausing momentarily, he looked directly at me and said "Please come to the front". His eyebrows scrunched and a certain look of annoyance was on his face.

"It's only my first day in this class and I'm already in trouble?" I thought to myself. I walked up to the front of the class and stood across his desk. By now, I felt as if the lights had dimmed and a spotlight shone on his face from above, Marlon Brando-syle in 'The Godfather'. I braced myself.

"So, you're the new student, huh?"

"Uhm, yes sir!", I said in reply to his *first* question.

His expression changed. It shifted from a frown to a smile in a few seconds. My anxiety level, which was already at Code Red, was now at Code Flamin' Red!

He continued —

"Do you know that the exams are in a couple of weeks?"

"Uhm, yes sir!", I replied to the *second* question. It seemed that my answers were now only limited to these three words.

"The students have been studying for this exam for a while now. You've just joined this class today." he continued.

"Do you think you can pass?"

I was taken aback by this *third* question. I paused. My brain had to process it. "Is this a trick question?" I asked myself. My brain was trying to find not just an answer, but the *right* one. If I said "No", what would he think of me? That I was not prepared, ready or even scared?

I went with my gut feeling.

"Uhm, yes sir?". It was more of a question rather than an answer.

He then smiled and chuckled. By now I was sweating profusely.

When he had finished, his friendly demeanor turned serious again. The frown was back.

"I *DON'T* THINK YOU CAN!"

There it was. The infamous five words that would change my life forever.

Over the next few days, the scene repeated itself in my mind like a boomerang clip. I started doubting myself if I could even do this exam. I knew what I had to do, but for some reason I just stalled.

Amidst all of this, there were two people who always had my back. My parents. They supported me the only way they knew how and that was through words. Slipping small notes of encouragement into my textbooks and on my desk, they reminded me of my potential, that I can achieve whatever I had set my mind to and most importantly, that "I CAN DO IT".

The five infamous words were now replaced by these four powerful words.

"I *CAN* DO IT."

I was back from the depths of hopelessness. I believed that I could actually do it and to add fuel to the fire within me, I was determined to prove my teacher wrong!

As I sat for my exams, I repeated the mantra —

"I CAN DO IT!".

Fast forward a couple of months, I found out that not only did I pass the exam, I had aced it!

You see, believing in our abilities is truly the foundation to living an authentic life. It means that we are living by the standards that we set ourselves, not the ones given by others. When a belief is strong, nothing can come in the way of that belief but when it is weak, another opinion can easily sway or diminish it. For us to live an authentic life, we must create a strong foundation in the form of an immovable belief in ourselves.

THE PILLARS - THE ART OF LISTENING

My journey to becoming a fully-fledged architect continued after high school. I was soon accepted to study Architecture at University and it was another big shift in my life. This time, I had traveled across the globe to Scotland, UK. If the early years provided a strong foundation, then this period of exploration and adventure became the pillars on which my authentic life was built on.

People often ask me how I started my journey to becoming a Life Coach. Looking back, it could be traced to a moment I had with a friend just after midnight in the cellars of an old Edinburgh malt house.

It was past midnight one winter evening and there were only a handful of students remaining in the design studio (a former maltings building). The final submission for the design project was only a few hours away later that morning. You could hear the faint sound of Jazz music playing in the background, and the smell of coffee lingered. As I was applying the ink strokes to my drawing, I heard a faint shuffle coming from behind me.

The shuffling was coming closer and closer. By now I could also hear short, heavy breathing. It was getting closer and louder until finally, the laboured breathing was directly behind me. "What the f*ck do I do?" my mind raced.

"F*ck! F*ck! F*ck! What do I do?!"

Now, I've heard several accounts of unexplained activities in this particular malting house, especially late at night. Scenes from 'The Exorcist' and 'Poltergeist' now occupied my prefrontal cortex. In an instant, I came up with a plan to grab my coffee cup and have a swing at 'it'. "OK, on three!" I said to myself. "One, two, th —"

"Hey Kamil!"

I froze. "What the f*ck?!"

"Sorry to disturb you", it continued.

The voice seemed familiar. "Patrick!" I said under my breath.

I turned slowly and there he was.

"Hey man! Sorry, I didn't hear you there!", I lied.

I was able to bring my attention back to where I was. My drawings. Coffee. Patrick. Phewh!

As I looked up, I noticed something odd. This was a guy who always had a smile on his face but tonight was different. No smile and he had his left arm down with the right one folded across his body as if nurturing a wound.

"How's it going?" I blurted.

Patrick paused, and then replied, "Good. All good". I sensed that it wasn't though. His breathing became heavier as he glanced at my drawings.

"How's your project coming along, man?". I suspected that whatever he was experiencing right now was related to the submission and wanted to find out.

"It's good. Good". His gaze was on the ground as he answered.

By now I was convinced. Even though I had my own work to finish, I decided to ask him about his work.

"Hey, I haven't seen your work for some time now? Tell me all about it!", I asked with enthusiasm. In fact, catching up with him was a perfect excuse to take a break!

Patrick raised his gaze and for the first time, looked directly at me since we started this conversation. I sensed a change in him.

"Oh, OK. I'll show you!", he replied, unsure if he should but decided to anyway.

We got round to his desk and he ushered me to a card model of his building. It was impressive! Lifting it around, he described the experience one would have when they were inside.

"How would you approach the building?"

"Why is it shaped that way?"

"Why were the windows placed in such a manner?"

"What would you see when they stood at the entrance?"

"What material would the building be made from?"

I was very intrigued and my curiosity led to asking more and more questions.

By now Patrick was in full swing explaining the details. It was like watching a real-life Doc Emmet Brown from the movie 'Back To The Future'; full of energy and excitement as he explained to Marty McFly his time machine!

After a few minutes, I could see that Patrick was close to his own self again. He later apologised for taking my time and admitted that he had initially come to ask for some help about this work. In the end, he didn't need any. He thanked me and we went back to our desks.

"What the heck just happened there?", I asked myself. Patrick had come over to ask for some help with his work but left without me giving any advice. I just listened curiously and asked questions. That was it!

You see, negative self-talk is common to us all, especially when fearing the judgment of others, needing their acceptance, and also approval. That night, everything came crashing down on Patrick at the last minute. He was shaken at the 11th hour and was no longer sure about his work. The same questions that plague us all from time to time of "Am I doing the right thing?" or "What will other people think of me?". Talking through his project reminded him of all the great ideas he had put into his work. All I had to do was to listen.

THE CANOPY - THE ART OF ASKING

In Architectural terms, the canopy or roof represents the topmost protective layer of the building. The canopy provides protection and shade from the natural elements, and is also the highest vantage point. From this location, you are able to view the surrounding landscape from a much wider perspective. As such, it is apt that the third lesson from my journey ends here. At the top.

One of the first modules in the Architecture school was a case study of past architectural works. The idea was to interrogate the building to understand the design process of the Architect.

The building assigned to me was Jacques Herzog & Pierre De Meuron's 'Stone House' in Tavole, Italy. Set in an undulating forest setting overlooking an abandoned olive grove, the building 'rises up' from the landscape as if it was sailing at sea; part submerged, partly exposed. The design was simple. Stone-gabion-inspired facades are set in a concrete frame. One of the best parts of this building was the panoramic view you get from the top floor, capped off by an inverted pitch roof. Instead of protruding upwards as a normal pitched roof, the 'Stone House' had it inverted. This meant that water can be collected in the 'valley' that it formed rather than pushed to the sides towards the gutters. It caught my imagination.

Ahead of my meeting with my supervisor one week, I had prepared all my work in good time. The drawings, write up and a scale card model. I enjoyed preparing all the material, especially the card model. I spent days and nights carefully measuring, cutting, and gluing all the elements together. I made sure the measurements were correct, that the cutting blade was always sharp, and that the right amount of glue was applied to allow the pieces to stick together neatly. The end product, in my eyes, was a perfect replica of the real thing.

I was ready.

The day had arrived and I sat with my supervisor to go through my work. Halfway through the session, he was silent and observed the model from different angles. He lifted it and spun it around looking from the sides, from the top, and even from the bottom.

He paused.

Looking puzzled, I could sense that something was bothering him.

What he did next formed one of the most valuable lessons I've learned not only in Architecture but in life. He reached out to the model, lifted it, looked at me for a split second, and placed it in the waste-basket next to me.

Yup.

It happened. I wasn't dreaming —

A few week's worth of hard work and late nights are now literally in the bin.

He then turned to look at me and said "Sorry, I can't think, I had to throw that away".

I was still puzzled. My mind was racing with numerous expletives. "What the f*ck!!!"

As you might imagine, I was filled with all sorts of emotions in one go. I was crushed, angry, frustrated, anxious. I needed answers! "Why?!"

I got them after the dust had settled. My supervisor later explained that what I had produced was a mere direct representation of the design, i.e. a copy. Focusing on replicating it 'verbatim' did not allow me to express my true thoughts and interpretation of the real building. It kept me in my comfort zone by not allowing curiosity to flow in questioning and interrogating the concepts and ideas that went into designing the building. Yes, I had created a piece which I was proud of, but that was about it. By being curious and engaged in continual questioning, I would have found my own answers, which would allow me to be more creative in interpreting the building by my own accord.

Wow! I did not see that coming.

What I learned that day changed me. I understood that through the art of questioning, a whole new world would open up for us. The answers we seek lie in the questions we ask. Understandably, it is scary to ask ourselves some challenging questions. We sometimes fear the answers we might get. It's much easier to avoid them and remain in our comfort zone. However, in order to live authentically, we must be courageous and ask them anyway to seek out our own answers.

OUTRO

One of the true blessings that life gives us is the opportunity to rewrite our story at any given time. For so long, I had this mentality whereby my life was linear. I would study, graduate, get a job, get married, have children, buy a car and a house, work, and then retire. I mean, there was nothing wrong with it and many people do live their lives this way. However, I had not questioned the validity of this story and asked "What *is* my story?". Moments of crisis forced me to ask some challenging questions about myself. I began to have a different perspective about my life when I was able to sit with those probing questions. "Where have I come from?". "Where am I now?". "Where do I want to go?".

The beauty of life is that we can die a thousand deaths only to be reborn each time. These so-called 'deaths' happen when we are able to open our hearts to expose the inner beauty that lies within us. We become reborn again when we take action to realign again with our authentic selves. It may take one moment of rebirth. It may take several rebirths. It may take none at all! The key thing is to understand that building an authentic life is a continuous process as one grows, learns, and yearns to become its authentic self. True death happens when there is no more hope and in accepting one's current story as their final chapter. Real-life happens when we accept that our new chapter can be written — any time we choose to.

ABOUT THE AUTHOR

KAMIL SHAH

Kamil Shah RIBA RIAS is an Architect and an Award Winning Jay Shetty Certified Success & Life Coach. He is recognised by Brainz Magazine for his creative and innovative ideas, contributions to mental health projects, and dedication in helping others.

In Kamil's chapter, he explores three key architectural constructs based on life lessons encountered during his journey through Architecture that he has used to build his authentic life. Although specific to his journey, he believes that these lessons are universal enough to act as "blueprints" applicable to anyone wanting to build their own authentic life.

Driven by his belief in the unlimited potential of every human being and coupled with an insatiable passion for helping others throughout the pandemic, Kamil founded Kamil Shah Success Coaching in 2020 and later the Kamil Shah Success Academy in 2021. Kamil is also a father and a husband. He currently resides with his family in Dubai, United Arab Emirates.

Website: www.kamilshah.com
Academy: https://academy.kamilshah.com
LinkedIn: www.linkedin.com/in/coach-kamil
Instagram: www.instagram.com/iamkamilshah
Facebook: www.facebook.com/academy.kamilshah
Email: contact@kamilshah.com

13
KRISTI NELLOR

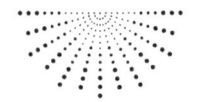

ENOUGH IS ENOUGH.

We just sold our beloved house on a coveted street in the East Bay hills for a lot less than we anticipated. We didn't have to sell it. We could have waited—paid the mortgage, property taxes and upkeep to relist it when or if the market bounces back. We could have rented it, kept it as an investment and pulled it's equity to buy a new house or paused on purchasing altogether to become renters for years to come. We had a lot of options in front of us, yet they all felt like a shit sandwich we didn't want to take a bite out of. The texture, taste, and wilted lettuce was enough to turn your stomach.

Dream. Believe. Trust. Receive. Seems so simple. It is, yet it totally isn't. Just when I thought we were getting it all together—the path was clear for my kids to be happy and provided for socially, emotionally, academically, and all the other ly's you can imagine, we moved. I had worked hard to set them up for success, giving myself fully to the endeavor. Jumped in with the gusto of a puppy's teeth on the wooden leg of a beloved designer chair. I mothered like I designed... with full intention, creativity, and everything I had. I held jobs filled with backhanded compliments on my unbridled creativity that made me question my self worth, but dammit, I had time for my kids. I had provided the roadmap for them to live their best lives so I could finally unleash my own. Between the demands of work calls, sports practices, and the ever present weight of holding the emotional equity of the entire family I dug deep and carved out little moments of space to delve into the crux of my soul. It was hard to listen. I didn't like a lot of it. But there was something underneath that caught my eye and I wanted to uncover it. For a long time, I had no tangible proof anything was under there—just this uncompromising vision that I was a Phoenix rising. It was super weird...something I never told anyone about. But it has returned many times since I shifted from being a Creative Director in NY to embarking on the next season: who would I be, how will I mother, where is my purpose, my impact, and ultimately what evolutions am I open and courageous enough to receive and breathe life into. The Phoenix came to me so consistently that at some point, I had to stop judging it and try to find it's message. Meaning by way of a cliché. Couldn't it be something way cooler? A sort of wild alchemy or colored dust...but a Phoenix?! I dug in and found that the light that lived underneath was unique to me. By showing up authentically as myself, I was helping others. While I thought I was failing in those jobs, others thought I was living my best life. They were watching me; asking for tips, drinking up my words, interested in how I wrapped my children in the conversation and nimbly pivoted in a pinch. They were inspired by a creative lifestyle led by curiosity and the wild approach that life is an adventure. Just when I thought I was invisible, I realized that I was actually making a difference just by showing up fully. I got to be curious, intentional, creative, and real which delivered a lasting impact on others. If nothing else, I was authentic. They saw and felt it. This insight unlocked something new and I began to help others find themselves too. I had clients, I loved what I was doing, and I still had time for my children. I thought I had finally figured it out. I was in flow. I AM the Phoenix!

Then the pandemic laid us full out. I know, you're thinking "Oh damn, it's gonna be one of those pandemic woke me up to what is important stories..." Not exactly but, it's part of it as it forced us to move. To a new city—that isn't so far away from where we lived, but is actually light years away from where we were.

My husband had taken an opportunity to soulfully breathe life into a start-up that was neither certain nor stable. It was a courageous leap that I begged him to take. One that forced him to expand exponentially and validated my deep desire to help others see their own genius. I helped him craft that narrative and also drafted the manuscript for my own becoming through the realization that I had been coaching for decades without even knowing it. The power of story is that we are in command of telling it, then retelling it with a whole new meaning. It was working out phenomenally until, you guessed it, our good ol' friend, Covid shut down New Rochelle in NY while he was there to grow the company. In a matter of days, he flew home and the entire company closed its doors. Shuttered.

Shuttered, not to be confused with Shuddered. Although when you combine both meanings, it's a beautifully succinct way to capture exactly how it feels: Closed and trembling from fear.

Yep. It was just like that. For the first time in our lives, we were completely free floating, yet had the heavy demands of a mortgage, cars, school tuitions, our children's well-being, and all the normal costs and concerns of close to middle age life.

The job search began. In a pandemic. We envisioned the goal and strategized the intentional actions to get there. We crafted the story of why and the belief that it will come when we most need it to show up. We cried. Together and separately. In front of the kids and quietly into our pillows. We shed layers and built beliefs, asked for help and got vulnerable as fuck. We also created possibility. He designed his materials with soul and meaning; I reviewed and edited them. We interviewed. I mean he interviewed on Zoom, and I kept the house quiet for three to four rounds of calls over weeks while two kids were distance learning on separate screens, I was in an entrepreneurial incubator, getting my coaching certification through another screen, planning virtual fundraising events, making lunches, dinners, and running recess in the backyard daily. But I kept that house quiet, and he had a sanctuary in which to tell a compelling story. We got very close to losing everything we had, but somehow that Phoenix metaphor just kept kicking around and I never believed we'd actually turn to ashes. We shifted the story to celebrate that it was all happening for us, reminding us to slow down and live with intention; stay in the present moment and root into the power of belief rather than the loss of control. The mindset of it all was breathtaking, exhilarating. Even, dare I say, addictive. What is this new way of being? On paper it says we're screwed. In my mind, we are free.

FREEDOM

I didn't really like my house at all until the pandemic locked me in it. I started to see the beauty of the old girl. The structure of her safety and the bounty she provided. The lush and luxuriousness of her private, intimate spaces where the sun kissed our cheeks and hummingbirds stared us down into a pool of wonder. A space within which we were able to explore our dreams and the scary things that stood between us and them. She made me face my truth. I fell in love with my house in the pandemic in a way I never expected. That place called to my heart and allowed me to go on the adventure of a lifetime within the depth of my soul, to find out that the soul is the essence of all things and I have always had the superpower of narrowing in on it—in branding, Halloween costumes, relationships, events, and now—my own life. I've been afraid of that skill because it scares others. It's big and takes up space and I always worried that I would take up too much room and people would hate me for it. They'd be jealous and wonder why I deserve so much attention that took away their time to shine. I didn't want to hurt a soul, but it was becoming too painful to dim the light in service of my fear of what others would think. When I realized that by stepping into the light, I could help others rather than take away from them, I realized the true power of vulnerability, connection, and story. It gave me clarity and with clarity, I could be courageous. Everything we've ever wanted is on the other side of courage. We tell ourselves we could never go there but what if we could? We tell stories all day long, every time we meet someone new or decide we love or hate a certain food... but the story we tell ourselves when we think we aren't listening is the most potent piece in unlocking what we desire. It's the hardest narrative to change, but it is the game changer.

So how did we decide to let this precious, life giving, soulful property go for less than we believed she was worth? Why didn't we wait it out or use these tools of manifesting to bring us exactly what we wanted? To put it simply, we surrendered. I would not have made this statement two years ago but I've seen miracles appear out of thin air. There was an amount of money that we believed was needed to pull through the pandemic and I joked that if we could only just get that amount as a tax return, it might be just enough to see our way out of this mess. I faithfully send my materials to a professional every year and he had no idea we desperately needed a return this time. Not long after that submission, a tax return arrived matching nearly the exact number I had joked about. It was just enough. And in the middle of the pandemic when no one was hiring creatives, my husband landed an amazing job that actually saved us... it just involved a move that we weren't planning to make. Let's revisit paragraph two... I was finally living the dream and making traction, remember all that? My kids were settled, happy, and achieving amazing things. I loved my house. But somehow, I fully believed that taking that job was the next right thing. The decision was not from scarcity, but born of possibility. It held unknown truths and adventures that had no positive guarantee but I believed that whatever came, would be enough. It was to be a big move to another country... Canada. We rewrote the narrative that it was a last resort and instead felt deep gratitude for the opportunity to go on a new adventure. I surrendered the outcome and in doing so found a practice that would again and again surprise and delight me with not what I wanted, but what I needed. When our beloved house didn't garner what we thought, I was devastated. Angry. Embarrassed. I came back around to the power of surrendering and accepting the outcome that has revealed itself. It is enough. We have no idea what miracles or lessons are in store so we decided to focus on the dream of what we want to have instead of what we thought we needed. We thought we needed to sell at the highest value possible to be able to buy a new house right away, but the reality is, we don't even know what neighborhood we want to live in yet. We have time we didn't see. We literally changed our words to celebrate that it's happening for us, rather than to us, and that is enough to move forward positively. Yes friends, there are Jedi mind tricks going on here. What you are willing to see beyond what's visible is where the real magic starts to happen.

We thought Northern California would look a lot more like Southern California so we toyed with the idea of moving to LA a few times but were worried about uprooting the kids. Now that we were deep in the research of Vancouver life, we joked about how we wish this move would take us to LA instead. Maybe a month later, the opportunity to grow their design studio in LA was presented to my husband as an evolution of his original role. Out of nowhere, we were given the choice to move to Vancouver or LA! Just like that, we were back in control of the next step, switching from: you must, to: choose what is right for you. The only work was surrendering the outcome, saying yes to what was in front of us, being open, curious, courageous, and believing in possibility no matter how it shows up. Whatever it is, it will be enough. I have long been a skeptic but somehow, I found my way onto a spiritual path that opened my eyes to the power of story, thought, and belief in terms of our lives rather than just the brands I built. The very thing that attracted me to design was the thing that holds the power to change your own life. The power of story. The magic is in the mindset, the approach, the actual words you tell yourself. You are the storyteller in control of the narrative.

So, now we were in choice and decided to try each location for a month. It was an aggressive schedule so we booked two different places in LA that spanned over Thanksgiving. The mere thought of packing everyone up to switch houses in the middle of the trip was overwhelming, but it fit the budget and timing. Those plans were locked and loaded when I saw our dream house listed for a whole month stay. We'd shift to the month of December, spend Christmas and New Year's in a creative space where the entire house would be decorated for the holidays, there was a private, heated pool, and the house was modern, minimalist, and tricked out with the best furniture and art. It was a bit over budget, but you couldn't have dreamed of a better experience for us. We'd have more time off to explore and family could join us for a destination holiday! Cancelling the others meant losing big bucks that we didn't have and it was already over budget, so why even consider this?! Something was calling to me, so I wrote to the host and told her our story of job loss and relocation, my desire to make this trip meaningful to help our kids enter into the transition with ease, that we loved her design aesthetic, the Christmas decor would save my life, and I courageously told her it was over our budget and asked if there was any flexibility. I literally put my truth out there. She responded immediately, brought the price down, and told me that my story spoke to her heart. From there, a magical friendship was born, and I knew this was our house.

I agonized over how to make this happen and was angry that we were stuck. We couldn't afford to waste a single cent, but I couldn't let go of the idea of the experience of her house. There was an inner knowing that I kept talking myself out of because I couldn't see a logical way to make it all work. I went in circles. It had everything we needed, including a promise of a friend and support network, but I was stuck in the fear of money loss and crippled with indecision. My coach reminded me to believe that I could have all I dreamed of with ease. That I was worthy of what I wanted and to simply ask the other hosts to cancel and offer a full refund. Even so, AirBnB holds fees that they rarely reimburse and those alone were too much to bear. She invited me to ask for what I want and then surrender the outcome completely. This was the most woo-woo shit I'd ever heard, things like this don't just happen. There are rules and I agreed to them when I booked it! It was gut wrenching to work through my need for it to only turn out the way I wanted it to. I had to completely surrender and accept the outcome before knowing what the outcome would be; to be ok with paying money I didn't have in order to have the experience I knew we needed. I wanted to throw a tantrum but instead, I chose to surrender. With a shaky hand, I booked the dream house and with a shakier voice, I reached out to both of the other hosts. They filled the spots and miraculously gave me full refunds. Although AirBnB took longer, they also refunded 100% of the non-refundable fees. We came in right at budget financially but way ahead emotionally. When my kids walked into their rooms for that month, they found a Christmas present waiting for each of them from the host: special stuffies that made those beds feel like home. They sleep with them to this day. The morning we arrived, LA went into Covid lockdown so we spent countless hours in that house, in that pool, inspired by that art. I wrote about it, I dreamed beneath it, I found a deeper calling in my work and greater focus on how to help others unlock their dreams. That house had a soul that filled ours up when we needed it most. It was clear that LA was the place for us. We never took a trip to Vancouver. We were already home.

The move on the other hand, hasn't come with ease in the least but has given me clarity in the same way my old house gave me permission to explore my soul when I didn't even know I needed it. I prayed for clarity, purpose, and guidance. I thought it would come by way of another vision…but it showed up in the form of an experience that made me question everything. It has tested the very teachings that had opened my eyes to miracles. If I can manifest things that are beyond my wildest imagination, what did I do wrong here? Why isn't this happening with ease? Why did my beautiful house sell for so low? Why the cascade of disappointments? I know the tools to make unbelievable things happen so how did I get here? The truth is that the ending isn't written yet, but as I sit here in the backyard of our temporary rental, having just sold my house for less than I wanted and no clear picture of where we will live in a few months, I can honestly say, I love my life. It's raw, weird, and not comfortable, but it's adventurous in a way that doesn't look that adventurous at all. The magic is not in the extraordinary, even though that's what gets the attention. It's in the art of the surrender and unwavering belief that whatever comes, it will be exactly what I need. It is happening for me, and it is always enough because I am enough.

My family just attended the host's wedding in the backyard of that dream house. In the same space that we swam and dreamed, did morning yoga on the lawn, and decided to make our big leap, my daughter fulfilled a life-long dream of putting on a tiara and being a flower girl to witness another story in the making. The big leap of a special soul who we were meeting for the first time in person, but whose heart and story intertwined with ours to help us write the next powerful lines of our own narrative and whose friendship has been a life-line as we begin to settle in. This is exactly how the Phoenix rises time and time again in a beautiful spray of colorful dust and dramatic alchemy never seen before. She lets go to see beyond what is visible and courageously believes that what shows up is all there FOR her. She trusts that it will always be enough and she relishes the bounty of finding what she needed rather than what she wanted. Then she rises. With confidence.

Enough is always enough.

ABOUT THE AUTHOR

KRISTI NELLOR

Kristi Nellor is a Soul Consultant, Life Coach, and Creative Catalyst who helps you boldly find your voice one creative action at a time. Her decades-long career in branding has harnessed the power of storytelling to help hundreds of clients discover opportunities in everything around them and find the soul of their products and brands.

Through individual and group coaching, project consulting, and speaking engagements she utilizes that same process to provide a spark to see differently and a roadmap to help envision and achieve the epic life her clients often feel is out of reach. She truly believes the story we tell ourselves when we think we aren't listening is the most potent piece in unlocking what we desire.

Her wild adventure began in Kansas, took shape at RISD and Brown University, stretched onto Boston, NY, SF, and most recently finds her soaking in the LA sun with her two creative kids and husband. She is certain that the yellow brick road is the courageous path home...to the power of your authentic words, the bounce of your badass soul, and the courageous belief that you are enough.

Websites: www.kristinellor.com
Linked In: www.linkedin.com/in/kristi-nellor-1a584a1/
Instagram: www.instagram.com/k_nellor/
Facebook: www.facebook.com/knellor

14
KRISTINA BRUMMER

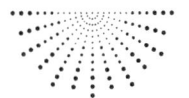

THE VIEW FROM THE MIDDLE

This past year I realized that putting the needs of those around me first no longer fit. I felt depleted and figuratively *out of breath*. Let me be clear though, I did this to myself. That perhaps sounds dramatic, so I want to share that it's not my intent to sound like caring for others was a burden, or I'm somehow deserving of great recognition for my efforts. The fact is, I self-declared my role to be that of putting the needs and wants of others around me first, whether they wanted me to do so or not. Then, when faced with a season in my life where the needs of others crashed up against my own, a conflict occurred. And, as a textbook middle child, an Obliger according to Gretchen Rubin's 'The Four Tendencies'[1], and an enneagram nine Peacekeeper, conflict is a state I wholeheartedly avoid.

Let me ask you, how many times have you heard the flight attendant's instruction, 'place the oxygen mask firmly over your nose and mouth — secure your mask first, and then help the other person.' My moment of realization I just mentioned was when I discovered I hadn't been listening to the instructions. (A very strange realization for a consummate rule follower like me!) What happened next was a conscious choice to put my own oxygen mask on first.

It was a weekday, and I had been working from home for almost a year since the WHO (World Health Organization) announced that the COVID-19 'outbreak could be characterized as a pandemic.'[2] My routine was to get up, make tea, wake up my daughter for her remote school day, get myself dressed, and head to my little makeshift office to log in for the workday ahead. However, on that day, something happened before all that routine rhythm; a pattern interrupt that shifted my life. I woke up, and I said out loud to myself, "I am quitting my day job and becoming a full-time entrepreneur." It was like someone else was speaking, but it was, in fact, and audibly so, my outside voice. I marched to the kitchen calendar, and I wrote on April 6th, in pen and, in big letters 'LAST DAY OF WORKING FOR SOMEONE ELSE.'

I felt a strength and power in my conviction and a triumph in the act of putting my flag in the ground. I followed up this personal announcement by going into my spouse's workshop and telling him, "I decided that April 6th will be my last day at my job, then I'm going to work full time for myself." His eyes did widen a little, but this declaration wasn't completely fresh news to him, so no panic set in. We had been talking about me leaving my day job to be an entrepreneur for over a year, but it had just seemed like a dream discussion. You know, the kind of flowing conversations that inspire you to create a Pinterest[3] vision board around a dream but one that you never actually set about doing the work to make happen. He replied to me with an "okay," and that was that. I appreciated his support and simple reaction, but I felt like I also needed some feedback about this declaration from someone outside my bubble. Perhaps to make it more real? So, I shared it with a friend over Zoom and had to wait only a nanosecond for her to clap her hands with joy on my behalf, pick up her pencil and say, "Okay, I've written that down and will celebrate with you on the day. It's real now." And so it was.

This feels like an appropriate time for my backstory, like in movies when suddenly the clothes, houses, and cars look outdated, and the hairstyles of the characters make you laugh out loud. So here it goes; cue the 80s hair!

BORN IN THE MIDDLE

I was born a middle child and felt like being in the middle was my birth gift. I say gift because I think the view from the middle is one that allows you to see the full spectrum of the landscape. You can literally see both sides of the image and are able to experience the whole and the sum of the parts. Sounds delightful, right? Yes, and not always.

Yes, my middle perspective means I see both sides to a shared story, but it also means I experience the pain when others can't. When two people can't see that they are speaking the same words and that they want the same thing from and for one another. Yes, I can see the whole picture and an abundance of choices, life, and colour, but that comes with a paralyzing pattern of overthinking each and every option to the point of exhaustion.

Being a middle child shaped my identity. I had an innate need to avoid conflict and create harmony in any and all situations by putting the needs of others first so that I felt okay. I made sure others were happy and cared for so that I felt okay. My birth position made me a natural mediator, a natural peacemaker, and a natural indecisive procrastinator.

You can see that it's not all positive and equally not all negative, but that's how life is designed. Think about these common phrases; you can't have a rainbow without the rain, a rose always has its thorns, and the dark comes before the dawn. Each phrase conveys that life is by nature designed with two sides; a yin and a yang. Life has a beautiful duality. A friend shared the idea with me that we will be our best when we learn to accept and flow with this duality, that we will be at our best when we stop resisting it.

PARENTAL INFLUENCE

Growing up, my parents said, "it's important to get a good job working for a company, and a government job is even better!" To their generation, corporate life was the golden ticket. It represented stability and security. The idea of the corporate ladder was drilled into my beliefs, and I packed my tool box full of administrative skills and got right to work climbing that ladder. Ironically, my parents were modeling the exact opposite.

My mom didn't work outside the home for the first ten or so years of my life. She was a homemaker and did mom-type things for and with us. She was the kind of mom who smelled like baked bread, had hands that were as soft as silk, and when she hugged me, the transfer of warm energy could be felt in every fibre of my being. When she did go into the work field, it was as a caregiver; a profession not far from her role as a mother. She was still caring for others, only now it wasn't just her own children and husband. She was caring for the needs of others. I saw this, and I took note. She encouraged me to be creative, to be cautious, to follow the rules, to do my best, and not disappoint people. She told me that I only needed to be myself and that I should be truthful and not fake, and on more than one occasion, she told me that if I stood up tall, I could be anything I wanted to be. I heard this, and I took note.

My dad was self-employed; a painter like his dad and grandfather before him. He was the provider, and he worked hard. He was the kind of dad who spoke with directness, who set rules and boundaries, and when he chose me for the Saturday trip in the truck to the city dump, he made me feel like I was the most important person in that moment. Self-employment was a legacy that chose him, and from my vantage point, it was one that seemed more like the shackles of responsibility than a purpose or a calling. I saw my dad work hard, and while he didn't seem to love what he was doing, he did it with integrity. I watched him experience the pain of rejection because he was self-employed and, according to traditional thinking, 'not a good financial risk'. And, while to me it seemed that my dad viewed his profession as a means to the end for his role as a provider, he showed up. He didn't half-ass things regardless of how he felt about it, but his needs appeared to come last. I saw this, and I took note. He encouraged me to work hard, to get good grades, to follow the rules, to do my best, and not disappoint people. He told me to act with integrity and that my word was my honour, and on more than one occasion, he told me to get a good corporate job, and a government one would be even better. I heard this, and I took note.

Our parents shape our beginning, and they give us some of the tools to navigate the middle and beyond. A sweet children's book was shared with me that says there is "An Invisible String made of love."[4] that connects our hearts. I know this to be true. It's the reason for that feeling you get when you haven't seen family or friends in a long time, but you say, "it was like no time had passed." You were connected through that string all along. My dad and I live in different towns now, but I never feel far from him because we are connected through that invisible string. My mom passed away from cancer when I was 21, yet, despite the loss of her physical presence, the connection and her guidance have carried on through that invisible string.

Obviously there is much more to my background, but these things reinforced my beliefs that my role was to; keep the peace, do my best, act with integrity, get a solid corporate job, avoid disappointing people, and be the caretaker of others' needs. I've navigated my life with this list in mind, and it has brought me an abundance of opportunities, rich experiences, and a steady flow of the most incredible people coming in and out of my life. Wait what? Right about now, you're thinking, why the heck did she spend time talking about being out of breath and in need of an oxygen mask when she sounds like she is living her best life? Well, remember that comment about the duality of life? I lacked oxygen because I took on all these things, like an athlete training for the Olympics. I was hardcore, and I got the most incredible rewards, but I also got hefty doses of fear, doubt, and anxiety, as I desperately tried to do my best and not disappoint people. Fear, doubt, and anxiety became the counterbalance to my rewards.

THE SHIFT

My early 40s was the start of my shift because I realized I had chosen to focus most of my energy on caring for others and inserting myself into their family units and hadn't taken time to create my own. This was the first time I made a conscious choice towards putting myself at the top of my priority list, by stepping out of my comfort zone and sparking my transformation. I met my now spouse and his daughter, and my own family unit was born. The balance to this choice was that when my energy shifted away from my family of origin, those relationships suffered a disconnect, and it was painful. I had put them first for so long, and now without warning or a transition period, I was changing the agreement. My choice hurt them and gave fuel to my anxiety, doubt, and guilt.

Shortly after moving to live with my family of choice, the next shift occurred. That stable, secure government job I had worked so hard climbing the ladder to get ended due to a corporate reorganization. If I'm honest, I wasn't happy there and had been weighed down by micromanaging bosses and the lack of freedom in the 9 to 5 grind for some time, but it was what I had worked so hard to achieve. It left me feeling off-course, like a boat without a rudder. I spent time asking myself what was next, and ideas about working for myself surfaced then. I shared those with my spouse, who was himself self-employed, but they were just whispers, and my foundational beliefs about job stability took over. I hopped on the first corporate ladder that revealed itself.

I worked the new corporate job for two months when I realized I had made a huge mistake not choosing a different path. It was the first time I regretted seizing an opportunity. All the stifling issues I had felt in my previous job surfaced faster than I could blink. I was disheartened, but my drive to not disappoint people had me course correct, pull up my socks, and do the practical thing; show up with all my work ethic in tow. There was a problem though, I was running out of oxygen again and could barely breathe.

The next shift happened by accident, literally. I was walking, fell, and fractured my left foot and right elbow. And the universe used my physical body to make a choice for me. My corporate grind was put on pause for more than a month. I was not able to work, and putting others first was just not an option because I was the one who needed help. I needed help washing my hair, getting to bed, and doing the most basic of tasks. I was not able to help others during this time, and it was extremely frustrating for me.

One afternoon during my recovery, I became so irritated by my hair being in my face that I tried desperately to put it in a ponytail, but with my one-handed status, it just wasn't working. I tried over and over until my arm hurt, and I cried in frustration. I paused for a moment of self-pity, then took that work ethic and fortitude I'd been gifted, and I did what any modern girl would do; I googled how to do a ponytail with one hand. I found a video of a woman who had lost her arm in an accident demonstrating how to do a one-handed ponytail. I was humbled by her, and after many failed attempts, a few more tears, and some physical pain, I successfully put my hair in a ponytail. It was messy and lopsided, but it was up and out of my face; I had met my own needs.

Over the next year and a half, my inner voice didn't let up. I added personal development to my toolbox, and I worked diligently to be present, to reflect on what I wanted, and to address my roadblocks, fears, doubt, and anxiety. I asked a lot of questions. How can I leave a stable paycheck and benefits and not end up broke and homeless?

What will others think of me? Will my family be disappointed in me? What if I fail? What if I succeed? Can we actually change who we are? With each question came more questions and seemingly little or no answers, but subconsciously the shift was happening. The very fact that my voice was relentlessly telling me that there was something more kept me asking the questions.

I became curious despite the fears of what might happen, and I suppose this was when courage came into the mix. I was scared to go against the beliefs that were so ingrained; get a good corporate job, care for the needs of others, do the responsible thing, follow the rules, avoid conflict, and for heaven's sake, do not disappoint people! But the status quo no longer fit. My fellow author in this book, Rachel Chamley[5], told me that my soul energetically grew bigger than my conscious mind', and she was right.

My spouse and I spent a year intentionally cleaning up our financial health, creating a cushion in case it was needed, and we talked as a team about my concerns and my questions. Having made the entrepreneurial leap for himself, he knew first-hand that it had to be felt, not taught, and he gave me the space to try and fail, to learn on my own, and to feel through it. I was still on the corporate ladder, but my spare time was acutely focused on becoming my own boss and on creating freedom of time, money, and location *for myself*.

Almost exactly one year before the publishing of this book, I signed my first client. She gave me an opportunity, and she believed in me when I wasn't quite there yet myself. That one turned into two, and then three, and I was on a roll, collaborating with amazing women who were on their own entrepreneurial paths, believing in themselves, putting their needs first, and experiencing their own transformations. I presented myself as a collaborator in their business, a partner to walk alongside them as they built, managed, and grew their business. After two months, I officially registered my business. I told people in my inner circle what I was doing and embodied my next level, which was an employee *and* an entrepreneur. Was my oxygen mask on now? Yes, and not really. I was burning the candle at both ends, working as a full-time employee and building an entrepreneurial business, and a choice had to be made.

That brings us full circle to my declaration on the kitchen calendar. I chose a different path for myself; I stopped resisting, and the six months that followed that LAST DAY OF WORKING FOR SOMEONE ELSE have been exhilarating, scary, challenging, freeing, and so much more. I have kept most of the things on my list; integrity, work ethic, a desire to care for others and keep the peace, and to be honest, a little of not disappointing people is still hanging about. What I let go of was the belief that a corporate job equaled stability and the one that putting my own needs first meant I wasn't a good, caring person. My family of origin, my friends, and my family of choice have all freely given me their support. Let me be clear though, I did this _for_ myself.

P.S.

Entrepreneurship is a roller coaster ride I like to call the Fear, Joy, Anxiety, Freedom Thrill ride! It is open to anyone regardless of height or age, but it has one requirement; you must secure your own mask first!

---

1. Gretchen Rubin, (2017) 'The Four Tendencies: The Indispensable Personality Profiles That Reveal How to Make Your Life Better (and Other People's Lives Better, Too)
2. Coronavirus Disease (COVID-19) Pandemic Timeline Article, https://www.euro.who.int/en/health-topics/health-emergencies/coronavirus-covid-19/novel-coronavirus-2019-ncov
3. Pinterest, Pinterest is a visual discovery engine for finding ideas like recipes, home and style inspiration, and more, https://www.pinterest.ca/
4. The Invisible String, Patrice Karst, 2000, https://theinvisiblestring.com/
5. Rachel Chamley, Mindset and Manifestation Coach, https://www.rachelchamley.com/

ABOUT THE AUTHOR

KRISTINA BRUMMER

Kristina is a middle child, a lifelong learner, a peacemaker and a lover of good conversation. She is also a daughter, sister, niece, aunt, granddaughter, spouse, mother, and friend; happily supporting and sharing in the lives of those she loves.

After a career of executive administrative roles, a shift happened and she is now the CEO of her own company, The Spectacular Middle Virtual Entrepreneur Support Services. Bringing her years of experience working behind the scenes to the forefront to collaborate with Entrepreneurs as they grow their businesses and activate their own CEO status.

In her chapter, she shares how she decided to put herself on her priority list, how being a middle child shaped her life, and how transitioning from employee to entrepreneur made her realize she had to put her own oxygen mask on first.

Reach out if you are looking to uplevel your business and claim your CEO status in a collaborative and strategic way.

Website: www.thespectacularmiddle.com
LinkedIn: www.linkedin.com/in/kristina-brummer-cphr-28695b112/
Instagram: www.instagram.com/thespectacularmiddle/

15
DR. LESLEY RIVERA DPT

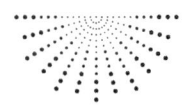

OUTSIDE LOOKING IN

I was in the second semester of my graduate degree. My daughter was six months old and my son was two and a half. With so little sleep every night and surmounting homework and studying, it was easy to think that every minute counted. So whenever my husband was at work, nap time for the kids was valuable study time for me. My daughter wasn't yet crawling, so I'd set her in a safe place while I would put my son down for sleep, and then I'd carry her around the living room and catch glimpses of my notes until she was asleep, then I'd settle in and study for an hour.

On such a day, I left my daughter in the play area, but I forgot one small detail. My son was potty training and I'd had his Mickey Mouse training toilet there as well. It shouldn't have mattered; my daughter wasn't crawling yet. But as I turned back to her, ready to snuggle her to sleep, there she was, sitting next to the potty happily splashing away. Did I mention that I'd forgotten to empty the thing too?

It's a lesson every parent learns. Things will often go awry. When you go back to school as a parent, these challenges can seem even bigger, partly because it feels like you'll never have enough time to keep up, and moreso because you're so damn tired. This is my favorite story of realizing my daughter could crawl. It was gross and I felt so dumb in the moment, but even then, instead of crying in frustration, seeing her happy face and the bath and snuggles afterwards, I just had to laugh. It was a perfect moment. A perfect reminder that there's no such thing as ideal hacks or schedules that will make going back to school feel possible. So why was I doing it?

"You're going to be alive for the next five years anyway. So you can either finish those years with a new career or not."

This was why. Because I wanted to be a Physical Therapist. Because it had been in the back of my mind for years, and I'd umm'd and ahh'd for long enough. These words were spoken to me by my friend Megan, and they were what I held onto when I finally decided to change my path.

I would describe myself as a woman of inaction. I spent years talking of grandiose dreams. I wanted to be an actress, or dance. Maybe be a CEO of a nonprofit that helps save the environment. Or own a coffee shop. Or figure out how to become wealthy because I want to travel and be comfortable. At the heart of it, I wanted to feel like I mattered. I am the youngest of three kids. My brother is incredibly gifted – a natural with the sciences with a work ethic to match, an artistic talent, and adventurous. My sister will try to tell you she is not gifted, however, a few minutes of conversation will quickly reveal how intelligent she is with a kind, supportive heart. As an adult, they are the two most encouraging people I know and I am proud to be their sister. But as a child, I got used to hearing that I was the "normal" child, or my personal favorite "wonderfully average". I heard these words, and similar words, from teachers, members of our church, parents, even friends. My brother went to a top school of science and engineering. My sister went abroad for university. I was told I had to prove a fancier school would be worth it for me.

So I took a sensible route in life. I went to community college because I didn't know what to do next. I have no regrets as that is where I began hanging out with Mike, my now husband, and Megan. I transferred from community college to university and majored in business. It was safe. I took opportunities that arose. In most respects, I was a successful adult. I did well enough professionally, my husband and I owned a small home and we squeezed in some travel. And somewhere along the line, like so many others, I knew I wasn't satisfied. I knew that buried deep within me was the potential to achieve some of my dreams, I just didn't know how to yet. Out of all of my random dreams, Physical Therapy stuck out to me the most. Physical therapy is a career where I could help dancers continue dancing, though I can't dance myself. It's where I could help a person after a stroke return to a hobby they loved. Or, my most prominent inspiration, it's a career that helps a person with multiple sclerosis, specifically my mom's best friend, continue walking decades longer than she'd expected to.

If I have this dream, why am I a woman of inaction? I took some baby steps, like talking it over with Mike and my sister. I started to sign up for classes, but I also dropped those classes because I couldn't be sure I was ready to take the risks involved. My husband and I had a mortgage to pay and wanted a family. We were approaching 30 years old. We could postpone having a child, and I could go to school, but then I would be over 35 and increase the risk of complications. We could have a child now, and one child would hopefully be manageable while I was in school, with the support of my family, but I would have to quit my job, halving our income while racking up student loans. While all this floated in my head, my husband took the next step for me. To even apply for PT school, you must have at least 100 hours of volunteering or working around the profession. As a nurse at a local hospital, he had friends in the physical therapy department and set me up to volunteer.

Well shit. Now I had to follow through at least on the volunteering. There's no way I can mess up his relationships. And goshdarnit, it's like he knows me really well or something because he was hardly surprised when I loved it and I moved from volunteering at the hospital to also volunteering in an outpatient clinic and found more to love. And while we debated about having a child now or later, and while I worried about the amount of time it would take to truly follow through, I had lunch with Megan. Again, I was faced with someone who knew me obnoxiously well and knew what to say to me. She put time in perspective, and this time, when I signed up for classes, I followed through.

This first half of my story I had to come to terms with. I am so lucky to have the external support I needed. I did not find the strength within myself. I struggled to believe I could do it. I just knew that I was surrounded by people who did know I could do it, and I had to try because I respected them and appreciated them so much. It hurts to know I barely trusted myself to do it until I started classes.

If motivational quotes are hard to believe, it doesn't mean you're broken. If you read about people who found their inner strength or the seed of belief and found a way to grow it, but you can't find your seed, it's OK too. Some of us just need that little bit of external support first. I needed someone outside of myself to push me.

I started pre-requisite classes. I got pregnant. I kept going with classes. I had my son and maintained a 4.0. I was doing it. I saw my potential. My sister, my friends, and my husband shone light on it and gave me support. Even our next-door neighbors pitched in with last minute babysitting when we were in a pinch. I applied for Doctorate programs. I found out I was pregnant again. I nearly quit. There was no way to do this with two kids. I got into school and decided I had to do it now or I'd never do it. Megan's words hung in my head.

During school is where I finally understood all those quotes about inner strength. "She believed she could, so she did." "Sometimes the bravest and most important thing you can do is just show up." "What you do makes a difference, and you have to decide what kind of difference you want to make"-Jane Goodall.

Sometimes more than believing you can do it first you just need to show up and the belief will follow. I showed up every day. On the first day of my doctorate program, my daughter was two months old, my son was two years old, and I showed up and kept showing up. Through sleepless nights, I somehow made it back to class. The entire first trimester I cried often, but I kept going back. I had a few missteps; I even failed an exam. But I also passed a lot of exams and realized I was still moving forward, and more importantly, I was doing it on less than three hours of consecutive sleep a night. By the second trimester of school, my daughter was mostly sleeping through the night and I began to sleep more consistently. By third trimester, I was learning the tricks of balancing kids and school with a little more grace. *Don't panic about studying at nap time – take a nap instead if you can. Flashcards can be a godsend – handy when you feel motivated to review and easy to toss in your purse. Teach some concepts to your kids –* seriously! It can be hilarious and very memorable listening to a two-year-old trying to pronounce zygomatic process.

Above all, I was having fun. The more classes we took with hands-on skills, the happier I was. I got to work with children with cerebral palsy in a ballet class. We had a "stroke bootcamp" creating games and activities for people who'd had strokes and were willing volunteers. We interviewed those with amputations. And then we got our first clinical rotation, kind of like an internship, and I was out in the world beginning to treat real patients. The work and the stress were worth it through and through. I worked with patients after shoulder surgeries, I worked with patients with low back pain, I worked with patients who loved me as a therapist and brought flowers and gift cards as thank you's. I also worked with a few patients who didn't really like me, and through it all, I still came home comfortable. I hung onto this first experience when we went back to classes. When my kids cried at me for not being home and the guilt rose, I clung to the experience of what it was like to work with patients. My second clinical rotation brought me to a pediatric clinic.

There I met the happiest physical therapists and occupational therapists I've had the pleasure of working with. So now not only was I enjoying the work, I saw people loving the career. The hours were great as well. I knew when I was going to be home, and I had a schedule with my kids. How much easier this life change was becoming with that glimpse of the future.

That was my next great lesson, that when I wasn't sure if the change was worth it, and my thoughts alone weren't enough, I could seek out people doing what I wanted to do and be reminded of the end goal.

Before I graduated, the coronavirus hit. We were sent home from school weeks from finishing our final trimester. We managed to finish with the help of Zoom. Although my final internship changed thanks to the virus, I was able to go to a clinic local to home with a kind, supportive physical therapist to guide me. It was there I had to face the other side of the virus. While my husband dealt with the Emergency Room at the hospital and watched stories unfold of how this virus hit, I watched people without the virus in pain face permanent disability as important surgeries were cancelled. Sometimes I tried to help patients through growing depression from the isolation of not seeing friends. And there was my inner strength. It had grown this whole time. I probably found it before Covid-19, but in this final internship, prepping to take my licensing exam, I had confidence in myself. I had improved my resilience to making mistakes, and I could see the difference I was making every day, even in the face of this pandemic.

Today I am a Doctorate of Physical Therapy. I look back on my adventure to get here. I have Mom Guilt. I missed a lot of my kids' earliest moments, and I wasn't always patient when I was under pressure. I sometimes wish my story included more inspiration that came from my own heart instead of my friends creatively pushing me. At other times I love that I had that push and that experience of just one step in front of another, regardless of my confidence. From a person who was always hesitant to step forward, that push was refreshing. My new inspiration is to hopefully help others with their steps and share what I've learned along the way.

ABOUT THE AUTHOR
DR. LESLEY RIVERA DPT

Dr. Lesley Rivera DPT, is a Doctor of Physical Therapy in Orange County, CA and founder of Crazy Moms Study – a growing resource for parents who are looking to pursue their dreams with confidence in themselves, their decisions, and their parenting. Her mission is focused on helping people stay who they are, whether it's a patient trying to get back to hobbies after an injury or it's a crazy mom, just like her, who wants to try something new and is scared of the impact to her family.

Lesley has an insatiable curiosity for what motivates others and how we overcome our fears. Pulling these together she finds the stories people have to share that inspire and support each other. Lesley is using her platform to share the lessons she learned as a mom earning an advanced degree and encourage others to share their experiences through her podcast and website. When not at work, Lesley can be found enjoying camping with her family, making mud pies, painting, and joyfully wondering if the messes created are more fun for the kids or for her.

Website: www.crazymomsstudy.com
Instagram: crazymomsstudy
Spotify: Crazy Moms Study

16
MARILUCY HERNÁNDEZ RIVERA

CONFÍA

As I tried to gasp for air, I felt his fingers tightening against my neck. The face staring back at me was one I'd never seen before. The anger in his eyes scared me more than the fact that I couldn't breathe, and for a moment I thought, "is this how I'm gonna die?" Seconds passed, what felt like decades, when he pulled back and let me go. I ran into the bathroom and locked myself in. I didn't know what to do, so I prayed, and I asked the Great Spirit to protect me and my unborn child. This was not the first time my daughter's father had been violent, but it was the first time he took his anger against me. After that incident, many questions were burning in my heart: How the fuck did I get here? How could I not see it? Did I not love myself enough? Finding the answers to those questions took me years. Mostly because I was living in survival mode after giving birth to my daughter and also because I was still mending the wounds of losing both of my parents before the age of 30.

While I write these words, the chatter inside me screams: "what will my acquaintances think about me?" "will my siblings dispute?" or worse, "what if the father of my daughter returns to retaliate?" At the same time, a soft voice whispers: "Take a deep breath, let the fear out. Your experiences, truth, and life are valid. You are safe to share them now." It wouldn't be authentic if I didn't voice what I know to be true and the lessons I've learned. As Maya Angelou said, "There is no greater agony than bearing an untold story inside you." So in this chapter, I will attempt to find those answers in hopes they can shine some light on you too.

I was born in Puerto Rico, a small island of the Caribbean. The youngest out of four siblings. I grew up with my sister and my parents in the town of Trujillo Alto. Our house was in a very quiet neighborhood of only 20 houses surrounded by mountains. At the top of the hill, the view of the Carraizo Lake shone with our sacred mountain range El Yunque, in the background. A sight that still takes my breath away when I come back home.

Since childhood, I had a different upbringing from my siblings because I was born with neurological and sensory disorders. My parents spent the first years of my life taking me to therapies and giving me treatments to improve these issues. I remember cringing every time I heard my mother telling the story because I didn't want to feel different from everyone else. My household was full of love and laughter, but it was also filled with many fights and hardships. My mom was a secretary, and my dad worked at a company printing checks. And even though they both had full-time jobs, they struggled financially and had to work side hustles to cover the bills. Most of their arguments would be over money, and I remember worrying about losing our house or other necessities at a very early age. Even with all their hard efforts, we were never able to make a family trip to Disney or Spain, which were my mom's dreams, or go to fancy restaurants except for special occasions, and the Christmas gifts became less over the years. However, their financial status never determined their character and spirit. My parents were incredibly rich in many other ways. Their creativity and imagination, passion for arts and music, knowledge of history, philosophy, religion, and the esoteric, their search for truth and meaning, their profound faith and compassion, and their deep connection to nature and the Great Spirit, were my source of inspiration and the seeds they planted in me.

From a very early age, art became my friend, therapist, and refuge from the fighting outside my room and the worries of our financial struggles. I spent hours making crafts, painting, designing houses, drawing, creating toys out of recyclables, or teaching my friends how to create some made-up art piece. My imagination was a very fertile ground with never-ending sprouts. Making up new spoken and written languages was one of my hobbies, along with collecting weird insects in Snapple bottles and precious rocks. I was the odd girl with weird interests, with a very authentic laugh, that would get laughing fits in the most inappropriate moments. I was bullied since elementary school for being considered 'different'. Thankfully, I always found a few amazing souls that would get me, and they are still part of the pillars that hold me together today.

My mother was a beautiful green-eyed redhead, full of life, laughter, and love. A great dancer with a beautiful singing voice who made everyone feel special. Unfortunately, she suffered long periods of extreme depression that would turn off her light. We were very close. 'Mami' was my protector, the only person in the house I talked to and trusted. Our home was clearly divided between my sister and father and my mother and me. When she was diagnosed with metastasis cancer at the age of 52, right after my Senior Prom, our whole lives transformed. I became very angry at her, 'How dare you get sick and leave me alone?' In my ignorance, naivety, and selfishness, I started treating her rashly. After numerous chemos and radiation treatments, she was bound to a bed with several tubes going inside her body to keep her alive. My sister and I would take turns each night to take care of her, and I would be the only one in charge of doing the difficult jobs no one else could stomach. To me, it was not a burden but my way of thanking her for all she did for me. The last few months of her life, she stopped talking and hid under her blanket, pretending that nobody was around. So I didn't get the chance to tell her how sorry I was for my attitude towards her in the past, and I carried that guilt with me for years.

An early morning in October 2007, the scream of my sister woke me up, "Lali, she's dying." I flew to her room in seconds to find her breathing forcibly with frightening silences between each breath. Her soft pink skin turned pale green, her pretty green eyes darkened and crystallized, and she no longer responded to her name. Her soul was already transitioning, and her body followed a few hours later. The moment she departed, I felt like my soul went with her. I recall spending that first night, hiding under my blanket just like she used to do, holding my breath for as long as I could, hoping to join her until I eventually passed out. Everything became a blur after that. I just remember wishing I was also dead, and that feeling lasted for months...well, years.

Her death led me to an identity crisis and an intense depression. Growing into adulthood without her affection, love, advice, and wisdom while still mending the relationships with my father and my sister was a very hard process. I felt so invisible and lonely without her in the house. The communication between me with my father and sister was non-existent. One day, they decided to spread a portion of mom's ashes in the ocean without me, and my already dispirited heart took it as a betrayal. The trust was broken, and I had no idea if it could ever be repaired.

College became the only thing keeping me going, but I had no sense of purpose or goals. I began to lead a precarious lifestyle, self-medicating and running from my trauma so as not to assume the responsibility that being the owner of my own life implied. I started numbing my pain with alcohol, marihuana, and sex. Spending most nights at the bars around campus, staying at friends' apartments, and not coming home for days. I was searching for the validation, love, and acceptance that my mother gave me and that I was not capable of giving to myself, wanting to be seen, appreciated, and needed. The wild rollercoaster ride ended in a psychiatric hospital, a turning point for me. I had hit rock bottom. During recovery my father told me something that will stay with me forever: "Lali, the good thing about hitting rock bottom, is that the only way is up." And up I went.

With a lot of humility and gratitude, I packed my life in two suitcases and flew to the United States, where my godparents awaited. From the kindness of their hearts, they offered me their home to have a place to start anew. I began working and taking care of myself. My godmother, the healthy, strong, inspiration of a woman that she is, convinced me to join her in her 4am morning jogs—talk about transformation for this night owl! We did a couple of 5ks together and signed up for a Half Marathon for Breast Cancer. We ran in memory of my mother, her best friend, wearing pictures of her in our shirts and having her angelic presence by our side all the way. It was a positive and exciting chapter in my life, but the truth is I never felt like I belonged there. Puerto Rico was calling my soul. I had to go back to finish college, and most importantly, try to build a relationship with my father, after all, he was the only parent I had left.

I'm happy to say that I accomplished all of those things! I completed my bachelor's degree with High Honors in Art History, and my father and I were able to heal the wounds we inflicted on each other. Surprisingly, we also managed to live the experiences that we always wanted to do as a complete family, and much more! We honored my mother's dream when he met me in Spain during my college exchange, and together we spread a portion of her ashes in the Tajo River in Toledo. 'Mami' was finally in her beloved Spain. Little by little, we began weaving the threads of our bond.

Dadaio (as I called him) was a very courageous man, a warrior in all senses. When he signed us up for a three-month long experiential workshop, he had no idea what he was getting us into. The things we learned, did, and experienced in that "spiritual and mental bootcamp" were so incredibly scary but healing at the same time that our lives were forever transformed. As our connection deepened, I felt I was healing parts of my relationship with my mother too, and my gratitude with the Great Spirit for that opportunity will never be enough.

A beautiful connection that existed between my parents and me was our love for creating art. My mother had blessed hands that turned everything she touched into something beautiful. A sweet memory of my childhood was spending nights creating crafts with her, my sister, and cousins. My father, on the other hand, was a box full of ideas, but his creations were more spontaneous and freer, the opposite of mom, who focused on perfection and harmony. Dadaio used to come at night tired from work and lay on my bed while I drew or painted at my desk. He never said hi or goodbye, but almost every night, I would expect him to come into the room to rest on my bed and just be present. Even though no words were exchanged, for me, it felt precious to have him there.

Nine years after my mother's passing, Dadaio went to join her in the Afterlife. My compasses to guide me were gone, but there was a glimpse of hope and purpose forming inside my womb. I was four months pregnant when my father passed away of pancreatic cancer. Because I did not want to transmit my sorrow to my child, I spent the rest of my gestation focused on not feeling the devastation of his absence. All my energy was concentrated on preparing for her homebirth and staying healthy. But the truth is, I had a very gloomy pregnancy. My daughter's father was mostly absent, and we argued all of the time. I was very alone and also afraid of exposing the truth of our relationship. I say jokingly now that he was the sum of all the bad choices and relationships I had with men from a lack of awareness and self-esteem. He really fooled everyone, including me, posing as prince charming when in reality, he was a very controlling, manipulative, and abusive man. I could spend another few pages detailing the mental, emotional and physical abuse I experienced for over two years, but I'd rather spare you the drama. What matters is that I left the toxic situation before someone else could get hurt, three weeks after giving birth, to be exact. Although I was completely terrified of being a single mother, I had enough reasons to go on on my own, my baby being the biggest one, and the other, knowing that I had two angels backing me up.

Two souls reincarnated the day I brought my daughter into the world, hers and mine. The mastery that is motherhood and seeing myself reflected in her mirror has been fundamental in transforming the narrative of my life. I was forced to look at my relationships and what remained to heal in them, especially the relationship with myself and the relationship with the Great Spirit. I started to make a list of all the stories I made about myself and questioned their veracity. Was I just a poor orphan who would never find her place in the world? Was I just a hobby for men who did not deserve to be loved? Did I really not know what I wanted to do with my life? And more importantly, What was my part in all this, and what can I do to change it?

It's easy to see the speck in someone else's eye but not our own—point a finger and blame others or our circumstances for our misfortunes. The hard work is in accepting our role in everything and looking within to find the answers. I had to practice a lot of patience, acceptance, love, compassion, and tons of forgiveness, mostly to myself. I had to be courageously vulnerable to confront the parts of me that I didn't like and neglected because I didn't want to acknowledge them. Only then could the real healing begin. I've been fortunate enough to meet amazing kindred souls on the path and to travel to other countries in Europe, North America, and Central America, where I've met teachers who shared their wisdom and helped me heal. I've also lived unforgettable experiences that completely transformed my perspective of life, like being part of several sacred ancestral ceremonies, which gave me answers to some of my questions. The sorrow led me to get closer to the Great Spirit and to redefine our relationship. To value and live each experience more fully. Appreciating every single moment and making gratitude a lifestyle. With each blow, I acquired new tools for my 'Healing kit'. Tools that keep holding me up when the going gets tough. What tools do you have on your 'Healing kit'? If you don't have one, this is my invitation to you to start one now.

Throughout my life, expressing myself in an artistic way has saved me many times from my own thoughts and defeats. The tools in my Healing kit have included a journal for keeping track of my thoughts, memories, and emotions, a sketchbook for doodling without judgment and unblocking my mind, acrylics and watercolors for painting, pastels, oil pastels, colored pencils, and markers for drawing whatever comes to my heart when I look within, and an array of different materials for crafting. By creating a tangible representation of the chaos, and sometimes nirvana in my mind, I've been able to keep my sanity, regain my faith and have clarity again. My creations are not always beautiful or happy, sometimes they are disturbing and ugly, because they are an authentic expression of what's going on inside. Life is about embracing duality and art is no different.

I've learned that the grief we experience when we lose a loved one will never go away, but that we grow around it and the space between is filled with acceptance, forgiveness, gratitude, and love. That it is in the stillness of our anguish that we can hear the Great Spirit guiding us, showing us the way. I have recognized that there is a beautiful 'Celestial Tribe', ready to attend us the moment we ask for help. I've learned that if you don't believe in something Greater than yourself, a Higher Intelligence who is in control of everything and wants the best for you or have Faith that overcomes all the adversity you are experiencing, then you have nothing to hold you up when your world is turned upside down. You will be like a shipwreck in the ocean. Because there will come moments in your life that the pain will be so great that nothing will soothe it, that the confusion will be so immense that nothing will make sense, or that everything you had planned will collapse in a second; and in that pain, confusion, or uncertainty, the love of the Great Spirit will be the only relief and sustenance for your soul. Therefore, *confía* (have faith), because you are not alone, you are taken care of, and you are loved. I want to assure you that it is possible to find your voice, head towards your dreams, heal your relationship with yourself, and rewrite your story. Because like a phoenix, we are capable of being reborn as many times as necessary.

ABOUT THE AUTHOR
MARILUCY HERNÁNDEZ RIVERA

Marilucy Hernández Rivera, better known as Lali, is an artist and art teacher passionate about all things handmade. A rebel at heart, Lali went to learn all different mediums of art. From mosaic to analogue photography, drawing, painting, jewelry, lithography, ceramic sculpture, she's done it all! And obtained a Bachelor's Degree in Art History with High Honors. She's a true example of the healing powers of art making and the creator of My Heart's Remedy. In her chapter *Confía*, she talks about how she was able to transform her life after losing both of her parents by age 30 and surviving an abusive relationship while being pregnant with her first child. She blossomed into her authentic self through arts and the continuous reflection, acceptance, forgiveness, and nurturing of her relationship with herself and the Great Spirit. My Heart's Remedy was born from her realization that art indeed was her heart's remedy to heal all the loss and trauma she's experienced. Through workshops and art classes, she's touched the lives of many, from children to seniors. She is on a mission to continue helping others express themselves and change their stories one art piece at a time.

You can visit her website: www.myheartsremedy.com
and Connect with her on
Instagram: www.instagram.com/myheartsremedy/
Facebook: www.facebook.com/myheartsremedyart
Email: myheartsremedy@gmail.com

17
MICHELLE SAVAGE

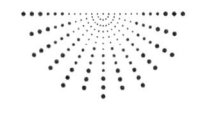

LIFE LINES

The first call I made to Lino was to tell him I'd be late. A bomb threat on the L-train severed my normal route between Brooklyn and the Italian restaurant I worked at in the East Village. Lino was too nice of a boss to give me a hard time, but I was scheduled to serve a large party that night and knew I was putting him in a pinch to set up.

I took a bus, then two different trains, and an hour later I struggled to orient myself to the unfamiliar street signs in lower Manhattan. Then, thirty minutes later I called Lino to tell him I wouldn't be coming in at all. Hanging up, I immediately dialed my best friend and roommate, Miriam.

"Hey!" I shouted exuberantly. "It looks like I don't have to work tonight. Do you want to go out?"

Sensing something strange in my tone, Miriam asked skeptically, "Where are you?"

"Oh, I'm in an ambulance. I was just hit by a car, but I'm totally fine. Actually, it was a little truck, but I can still walk."

I'm fine, I'm fine, I'm fine, I told myself.

"Yeah, she said, I think you better just come home after you go to the hospital. You're probably in shock."

Just a few minutes before calling Miriam, I'd exited the subway tunnel and realized I needed to take a taxi uptown. When the light signaled for me to cross the street, I hailed for an open cab.

As I stepped into the crosswalk, I heard a scream and felt the metal bumper of a pickup truck ram into the outside of my left knee and run over my foot. Defying the laws of physics, I didn't fall down and my body spun away from the truck like an invisible force was yanking me to safety. I stood in the street for a brief moment gulping for air in disbelief before limping to the sidewalk where I collapsed, laughing hysterically until the ambulance came.

In the days that followed the accident, my mind caught up with my body to survey the damage. I'd gotten off lucky with deep bruises, but the nerve damage ran up my leg and into my back, which led to a lot of painful physical therapy and, ultimately, the phone calls I hated making the most.

I called my choreographer to drop out of the dance performance I'd been rehearsing for and I called to cancel the rehearsal space I'd been using to choreograph my own production.

This is how it always seemed to go with me and dance—I'd leap two steps forward and some sort of cosmic vaudevillian hook would jerk me offstage.

And isn't that just how life happens? There you are chugging along, kicking ass, until one single thing happens that completely changes your trajectory. It's like there's an invisible line in time and once you cross over it your perception completely shifts and you are forever changed.

Change, of course, is inevitable and somehow we always end up where we're meant to be—either through dumb luck or conscious choices, but especially because the divine universe works its tail off to ensure our souls leave here a little less belligerent than when we arrived.

As a young adult, there wasn't a well-worn path I didn't try to avoid. I wanted to blaze my own trail, even if it meant scratching up my legs with stickers and burrs. My teenage son is the same way with a strong mind of his own and we jokingly call him the habitual line crosser. But that's the thing about lines; they can pen us in or move us forward, save us from drowning or wrap around our necks at birth.

Most of the lines I've crossed were worth crossing, if not because I came out winning but because I went in swinging and discovered my edge through my own experience rather than from the well-meaning advice of others. Sometimes you've just got to see for yourself what happens when you mix pot with three top-shelf cosmopolitans.

I do feel a bit sorry for the angels who were assigned to keep me safe in my 20's. *"Pssst...is this the HR department in heaven? In case you haven't been keeping track (and I'm certainly not questioning your accounting abilities), I'd like to point out my angels have clocked substantial overtime hours and are probably due for some paid leave or at least some wings in XXL. You'll see I'm right if you rewind the tapes."*

∞

I was eleven when my family moved from Montana to Virginia and as a way to sweeten the deal, my parents promised to enroll me in ballet classes. I'd been pleading with them to let me dance since my best friend invited me to watch her class—mesmerized by the sea of pink tights contrasting sharp against black leotards, and the piano accompaniment alternating between lilting sonatas and energetic staccato tunes.

At eleven, I was a late beginner and was placed in a class with much younger girls. A pubescent pre-teen who didn't know a plié from a grande jeté, I moved like a clumsy, lumbering oaf, always a beat behind the music.

My teacher gave me drawings of all the ballet positions labeled with their French names so I could practice them at home and my house became my second studio. The tall backs of our oak dining chairs were the perfect height for practicing bar exercises. I blared a cassette tape of Vivaldi or an Enya CD into the smooth, oil-stained concrete of our two-car garage, where I'd practice the adagios I learned in class.

The line between dedication and obsession blurred and within two years of diligent practice, I worked my way through the class levels and into the company, where I landed the role of Snow Queen in the Nutcracker.

From there, I auditioned at the Kennedy Center in Washington D.C. where I was awarded a place at Dance Aspen's summer program and was invited to Interlochen, a prestigious school for the arts in Michigan.

By fourteen, my dreams of becoming a professional dancer were already coming true. I could see the path I was on would land me in a top New York ballet company by the time I graduated high school, and there was nothing I wanted more.

Adding to my satisfaction was the fact that after wriggling around in the drama of middle school girls for the first two and a half years in my new home state, I finally had a solid group of friends, and met my first true-love boyfriend.

But then, my freshman year the school district re-drew the lines and I was bussed to a high school without any of my new friends. It was a rougher, dumpier school where fights were common. Being a tiny ballerina with long blond hair who'd been trained to walk like a duck with a stick up my ass earned me some unwanted attention from older boys who cat-called to me in the hallways.

Dance was the one thing that kept me focused and hopeful. I still had my secret life after school where there was an order to things and set expectations, and beauty.

It was on a cool winter evening in January when I moved over a line in time that picked me up and flicked me over the fence to a place I didn't recognize. As my true-love boyfriend and I ran around a grassy hill in his front yard, laughing and flirting, I stepped into a divot and my foot twisted sideways. It hurt a bit at the moment but I was able to get up and walk it off.

I'm fine, I'm fine, I'm fine.

The following day, some bruising appeared on the top of my foot near my ankle and it hurt to walk. By then, I was no stranger to pain and the art of pushing through it. I'd danced with feet so raw and blistered they bled through my pointe shoes —a badge of honor as I saw it. Whatever this was, I could take it. *I'm a Savage and Savages don't quit*, I told myself.

When I returned to class, I wrapped my ankle and took my position at the barre but I couldn't make it through the warm-up. My breath caught sharp in my throat as I pliéd in first position and couldn't fight back the tears. For weeks I toggled between rest days and trying to make it through another class, but each time the scene repeated— talking myself up, crying from pain and failing to make it through.

When our orthopedic physician told me I would never dance on pointe again, my internal bargaining was over. I was out of the company and ballet became something I used to do.

With one wrong step, I'd lost my superpower. Dancers can do things normal people can't do while making it look effortless. Unlike dancers who leap high and land softly or turn out a leg with perfect rotation from the hip, regular people only have access to linear, pedestrian motions that keep them moving like the descendants of apes. Lying on this side of the fence, I'd crossed over from dancer to ape.

Without dance, and relegated to a school away from my only friends, I curled in on myself. Compounding my sadness, my true-love boyfriend cheated on me with a girl from his school and broke my heart. Without love or friends or dance as my buoy, I began sleeping through Algebra and sneaking out at night to drink with kids from my school.

One month later, my mother crossed over a line that took the whole family with her. When the phone rang, I ran to stand by her side, straining to hear what the doctor had to say. No, the numbness and tremors were not the results of a brain tumor or Lupus or cancer—three of the four possibilities they'd tested for. Instead, at age thirty-nine, my mother was diagnosed with multiple sclerosis. Lesions grew on her brain and spinal cord as her immune system attacked itself, eroding the myelin sheath that protected her nerves. With shaky hands and fingers that refused to cooperate, she had to quit the only thing she loved more than her family—her job as a sign language interpreter.

The news of my mother's illness rolled in like a freight train, flattening my family under its heft and unrelenting momentum. Do people die from this? Which of the four types of M.S. does she have? Will she be bed-ridden in a year? Is there medicine for this? My mother's doctor wouldn't dare to predict the future and so the answers to many of these questions were on a wait-and-see basis.

When my dad was offered the option to transfer to a different sales region within his company, my folks decided Texas would be our new home. After the school year ended, we moved to Dripping Springs, Texas.

In a new high school so small my graduating class had only 140 students, I rode out the rest of my adolescence running track, making a few friends here and there, and gathering around kegs of Miller Lite in the dark. I bided my time waiting for the moment I could sprint to the freedom I imagined was on the other side of the line called childhood.

Not exactly landing in the *Dead Poet's Society* of colleges, my low SAT scores awarded me admission to Austin Community College. ACC felt no different from high school, other than the blacksmithing and art metals classes I enjoyed taking in the massive workshop on campus.

On weekends, I worked at a wild game restaurant where bacon retrieved me from a half-hearted attempt of being vegetarian. And in one semester, I gained twenty pounds in pheasant tostadas and booze.

One day after class I flipped on the television and the movie Flashdance was on. I'd seen it before, but this time was different. Watching the dancer on the screen go from her welding job to her dancing her heart out, I found myself sobbing.

I can weld things, I thought.

Damnit, I want to dance again!

That night, the Yellow Pages led me to my first beginning modern dance class where, once again, my clumsy ape body lumbered through the steps. I was sore before the class ended and I knew deep in my heart that I was regaining my superpower, barefoot this time.

∞

As soon as the words elbowed their way out of my mouth, I knew they were true.

"I'm not going."

I said this quietly and to no one in particular, but the chatter around the table quickly hushed.

The notion of not going to Spain was as much of a surprise to me as it was to all the other women in my family. There we were, on retreat in the Hill Country, playing in the river, sitting under the Live Oaks and sharing meals at the large communal table. I hadn't meant to drop a bomb on it, but the words just came out.

A few days earlier, as my then-boyfriend Brian and I tidied up the last details before our big international adventure, he told me he loved me but wasn't *in* love with me. This piece of information would have been helpful to know months earlier. Our plan, if you can call it a plan, was to stay at a house-sitting gig in NYC for two weeks and then go to Spain indefinitely, where he'd teach English. I can't exactly remember what I planned on doing, other than waitressing at a quaint sidewalk café where I'd instantly become fluent in Spanish and wear cute flowery aprons. But hell if I was going to follow a boy to another country when we had no future together.

The night I told my family I'd be forfeiting my ticket to Spain and was moving to NYC to dance instead, I had the most vivid and visually spectacular dream of my life where I was surrounded by enormous, monarch butterflies. Their speckled golden wings flapped in slow motion around me and I was filled with a warm sensation of peace. As a symbol of transformation, these butterflies seemed to show up to give me some cosmic high-fives and wish me well on my journey.

After breaking it to Brian he'd be traveling alone from NYC to Spain, I took a one-way flight to become the one thing I'd always dreamed of —a dancer in New York.

New York City is a magical place where the energy of the city slides under your skin, animating every molecule within you at once.

On my first two days in New York, I walked for hours mapping my way through the numbered and lettered grid of the city.

I was flying high with excitement, but also recognized I'd moved there with no job, no friends, no place to live and very little cash. With just two free weeks in a borrowed apartment, I dedicated my third day there to finding a job.

The first restaurant I applied to was a 24-hour French restaurant just two blocks from the apartment. I was hired on the spot and started working that night.

With time running low to find a permanent place to live, things began unfolding for me like my life was a divinely guided tour.

At work, I met a guy who needed out of his lease and I met a woman who was also looking for a new apartment. Pulling cash off my credit card to pay my part of the deposit, she and I moved into a sixth-floor walk-up in Soho.

Dancing in historic studios with world-class instructors was even more incredible than I'd dreamed it would be. And at night, I'd crawl through my bedroom window onto the fire escape to gaze at the lights on the Empire State Building. My eyes welled with tears more than once realizing that after all the false starts and crooked paths I'd taken to get there, I'd finally made it.

∞

I lived in NYC and danced in small productions for a total of six years and at some point, I stopped gawking at the city and became part of its beating pulse.

Getting hit by the truck only pressed pause on my dancing career, and after recovering, I performed for several more years. At 26, I married my choreographer, and two years later we had our beautiful son.

Year after year, the train of my life continues clackity-clacking along, rolling by the signposts that let me know when I've entered into new territory.

A move back to Austin.

A divorce.

Becoming a single mom.

Co-parenting.

Online dating.

Meeting my husband and his children.

Blending our families together.

On, and on it goes…a divinely guided tour made up of the things I consciously pick coupled with a destiny so great, there's no way I could have planned any of it.

Now, in my 40's, my love for dance has been replaced by other pursuits. I no longer care to lift my foot overhead or to see how far I can do the splits. Still, if you catch my ape body in the right light, you just might notice me pointing my toes as I reach for something on the top shelf. But this time, instead of leaving my superpowers behind me, I decided to carry them around inside.

ABOUT THE AUTHOR

MICHELLE SAVAGE

Michelle Savage writes because she's far too curious not to find out what will show up on the page.

In her chapter, Life Lines, Michelle chronicles her relationship with dance - how it lit her soul on fire, crushed her more than once and showed her who's in charge around here. Hint: it isn't Michelle.

Michelle has a B.A. in Cultural Anthropology with a Minor in English from the University of Texas at Austin and has been writing professionally for 12 years. As a writer, editor and content strategist, Michelle helps authors and creative entrepreneurs tell their best stories and build dynamic online platforms to supercharge their impact, create a loyal following and build a life a business that feels too good to be true.

Connect with Michelle!

Website: www.michellesavagewriter.com
Instagram: www.instagram.com/michellesavagewriter/
Facebook: Michelle Savage Writer
www.facebook.com/MichelleSavageWriter
LinkedIn: Michelle Savage
www.linkedin.com/in/michelle-savage-43032659/
Email: michelle@michellesavagewriter.com

18
OSWALD PEREZ

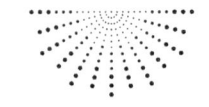

A FOUND POET

How my story began is the subject of family legend. I was born on December 1, 1985, at Flushing Hospital, just minutes after my twin sister. Six weeks earlier than planned and weighing 2lbs 7oz. My parents watched other babies in the NICU passing away around us and didn't think that we would make it. But by grace, we both survived. Even when I'm berating myself over the tiniest thing that goes wrong now, I always remind myself of that fact. This moment in time would only be the beginning of a long series of fights to occur throughout my lifetime. I'm more of a survivor than a warrior or fighter.

I didn't realize how much I had been through during my childhood. Recently I found a stack of my old Individualized Education Plans in one of the cabinets in my parent's room. Reading through them brought a much needed sense of clarity. My diagnosis was the mildest form of cerebral palsy. There were physical tolls, namely walking with a slight limp. And the mental ones, from being overly dependent and sensitive to being unable to tolerate failure. The photo of me with both legs in casts and all the orthopedics used. I was oblivious to it all due to being so young. It was as if my story had been written by everyone else but me.

Subconsciously, I was aware the whole time of all the things that made me different, in every moment of being made fun of for my body. "Bucktooth Beaver" and "Stinky Boy" were among the insults tossed around. In every pair of eyeglasses that I wore to protect a blurred left eye. And all the tears shed over little things that seemed big to me. Instead of running from them, I embraced my quirks.

I also noticed I had something special—the gift of wordplay. During middle school, I would write notes in the cards I gave my parents for Mother's Day, Father's Day, and their respective birthdays. I saw that they enjoyed the messages I wrote to them. It was the first sense that I, in fact, had something to offer the world.

As my sense of wordplay was progressing, so did the surgeries I underwent. The one in September 1996 that didn't take. Then another round in the summer of 2001, as the last round of surgery scheduled, turned into two surgeries in the span of six weeks.

I woke up on the afternoon of July 11th, 2001, in a blue cast that held nine stitches and three pins in place. For the next three days, I overlooked the East River from my hospital bed at the Hospital for Special Surgery with my parents at my side. The hospital discharged me on Saturday, the 14th. My days were spent in bed, unable to move without help. In so much pain that taking the first prescription of pain medicine was done in short order. I was at my lowest point.

Things began to turn around. My sister came home from her summer program the following weekend, turning my despair into joy. I started walking again with the help of a physical therapist coming to the house twice a week. My strength was regained just in time to go under the knife a second time on August 31st.

With both surgeries finally completed, my long road towards normality began. It was at a snail's pace as I started my junior year of high school in a wheelchair. Returning to life as a regular student after years of being taught in special education programs was another challenge to be faced. Twice a week after school for the next nine months, I would go to the Hospital for Special Surgery to continue rehab on my leg.

As time marched on, I began to lose the assistive devices. Goodbye wheelchair, then walker, to only a cane, and then a brace on my right leg. It certainly wasn't the easiest of school years, but I made it through.

Then along came the magical day in August 2002 when my surgeon said the magic words, "you can take the brace off now." With a dumbfounded look on my face, I removed the brace and took my first step forward. As I took step after step, a beaming smile of pride came over me. All the struggles of the past faded away in that one moment. I felt reborn.

Excited to return to school my senior year in September 2002, I couldn't wait to show my leg off to everyone fast enough. I felt free for the first time in my life. Little did I know, a second rebirth was about to happen. During English class one day, my teacher Ms. Levy, gave us a homework assignment. We were given a list of words with the objective to turn them into a found poem. When I received the paper back a day or so later, I noticed something written on the left margin. The words, "Oswald, you are a poet!". This designation didn't resonate with me at first, as all that mattered to me was passing my Regents exams and getting my High School diploma. I wouldn't grasp the significance of this particular moment until I came across a blue folder with rough drafts of pieces written from that period of time much later on in my life.

I stepped away from poetry and gave blogging a try. As I began my studies at John Jay College of Criminal Justice in the fall of 2003, I began to write about life as a college freshman. I didn't write for a particular audience, simply to document the days as they went along. It didn't last long as I shut down the blog after a time. But it wouldn't be the last time that I'd turn to writing as a means of expressing myself.

As the years went by, I was further inspired to give other forms of creativity a try. There was a brief playwriting phase. I would visit the drama section of Borders Books in the Time Warner Center in between classes. As I read the books, I would think to myself, "maybe this is something I could try." So, I set about writing short plays as I looked into the crystal ball to catch a glimpse of what my future might look like. Writing during class lectures, I daydreamed of my life as an adult with a wife, kids, and a job that I loved. Though I desired the job to be in the travel industry instead of criminal justice. With no specific direction in mind to do with what I had written, I typed up the pieces and shelved them far from sight. Once again, I put my writing on pause to finish up my Bachelor's Degree and begin my job search.

It would be another four years before the urge to write came back. A bit of luck was involved. In May 2012, I won a pair of round-trip flights to Paris via Time Out New York and XL Airways France. Coming off a disastrous job interview, this moment was the ray of light I needed. In October of 2012, my sister and I took a weeklong trip to Paris, adding on a weekend stay in London. This was the first time traveling without our parents. While sightseeing, I had a few close scrapes and some more lucky breaks. I learned the hard way that I can't have seafood after eating lunch in Versailles. Anchovies in the caesar salad caused my face to swell and my eyes to go bloodshot red. Thankfully, I recovered quickly enough to make it up the steps of the Arc de Triomphe later that night. The next evening, I overdid it during a wine tasting. Not enough food and six glasses of wine came back up to haunt me at the end of the night. I soldiered on for the rest of the week. I didn't want the trip to end, thinking that I wouldn't travel internationally again for a while. The morning of October 15th, as all of the memories of this trip came flooding back to me, I wrote one long and rambling Facebook post. After the guilt and shame of realizing how out of sorts I was and being concerned I said too much,

I checked the comments of that post. One of them said, "you should write a blog." I took this as a sign to return to blogging.

I was slow to embrace this return to writing. When the time came in May 2013, at the advice of a friend, I christened my second blog, "The Blog Underneath The Security Blanket." The last part of the title kept coming to mind as I am a big fan of the Peanuts comics. The phrase "security blanket" would come to identify the means that I would hold onto the past instead of letting it go and embracing the present moment.

The blog's return also coincided with movement on the job front. In the summer of 2013, I began as an intern at the organization I still currently work for. I helped organize donation receipts, tag clothing, and type up documents for the four months that I worked in the warehouse. I finally felt like I had found a place where I belonged after every other prior assignment had gone astray. Though I knew it wouldn't lead to a permanent job in the end, by the time I left, I felt as if I finally belonged somewhere.

Serendipity always has a way of making itself felt. In November of 2013, I was tipped off that a position had opened up in the call center of that organization. After a string of misses, I had to apply for this job as it would be my best shot at being employed. I had the best job interview of my life in December with the entire warehouse crew cheering me on. It was to no avail as I didn't get the job. Or so I thought.

It turned out I would work my way up the ladder as time went on. From being hired temporarily for two weeks that January and returning in March on a part-time basis. All the while starting from ground zero—learning how to take calls, schedule donations, and process insurance documents. Then one day in August, it happened, I was offered a full-time job. It was another moment of rebirth for me as the six years of struggles trying to find a job faded away.

My first year at work was a struggle. For all the skills that I learned, I still wasn't prepared to handle the new life in front of me. My sensitivity became a liability as to the more aggressive the person on the phone making a complaint was, I found I would respond in kind. I was able to make it to my first work anniversary in January 2015.

Another moment of rebirth was coming up. Early in 2015, I found out that my sister and her friends were heading to Hawaii to celebrate our 30th birthday. I couldn't go as it was a girls only trip. I told my sister I wanted to travel on my own. She advised me that escorted group tours would be the best fit. After visiting Paris and London in 2012, I wanted to return to Europe. As "Don Quixote" came to mind in considering my destination, I decided Spain it would be.

There was a bit of anxiety as I arrived at Terminal 8 at JFK Airport in November 2015, as my departure was only two days removed from the attacks in Paris. However, I knew how momentous this trip was going to be for my growth as I was traveling alone before meeting up with the group in Madrid. I felt an immense sense of pride as I paid for this trip with my own money as opposed to cobbling it all together three years earlier. There I was the next day, standing on Kilometer 0 in the Puerta Del Sol. From "Guernica" and Toledo, to the Alhambra and flamenco. The eight days that followed with a bus full of people embracing me as the only solo traveler proved that I could truly stand on my own two feet.

The years that followed took on a familiar beat—work, live events, and more travel. Colleagues came and went, with the circle of friends simultaneously shrinking and growing. Toronto, Barcelona, San Francisco, Dublin, San Juan, Lisbon, Nice, and Mexico City were among the places visited. I kept blogging and occasionally writing poems. Despite being told how good my writing was and that I should write a book, I didn't take it seriously. For all that I've accomplished, I still felt as if nothing was being done except getting through my days. All of that would begin to change with the start of a new decade.

Another moment of serendipity arrived on a Sunday afternoon in January. After completing the 20/20 Vision Challenge from Cathy Heller, I signed up for her signature program, Made To Do This. I was at the New York Times Travel Show when an offer arrived in my email. I took it as a sign from the universe that it was time to finally take my writing seriously. The opportunity was much more important to me than the money. As I sat at Little Mercado Spain later that day with a glass of Mahou beer in hand, I pondered what I was getting myself into.

The next 12 weeks would push me into another uplevel. It was a slow go at first. I was so self-conscious about everything that I did. From being afraid to be on camera to not having my "thing" (business idea) sorted out as soon as everyone else did. The thing I did do was to keep on keep writing.

Everything changed on a Sunday night in March. At 10 PM on the 22nd, I was the one called upon for a 1-on-1 hot seat coaching call. I panicked as the zoom chat blew up, to the point that I wanted to run from the moment. A pair of friends wouldn't allow the moment to pass me by. By the end of the conversation, a new mantra took hold: Words Are Art! My first post the morning after with this new mantra surprised me with the level of reaction. I realized that maybe there's something to what I am doing after all.

I needed to build upon the momentum of that moment. I finished the program without a tangible offer. A suggestion was made that I should publish something to set the course for the back end of 2020. I would send out a manuscript that would become the foundation of my book, "A Poetic Journey, Staying At Home".

At long last, the day arrived! Tuesday, October 27th, 2020. The long, winding road led to the release of A Poetic Journey. As I reveled in the spotlight, it wasn't lost on me how much it took to get here. I recall the journey each time I turn my head back and view the promo poster hanging on my bedroom wall behind me.

What does the future hold for me?

In a year's time, I hope to begin a long-awaited 12-day tour of Italy. I can already envision the scenes of a sunset overlooking the Piazza San Marco in Venice, Michelangelo's "David" in Florence, the alfresco in the Sistine Chapel in Rome above my head, and the deep blue seas that surround the island of Capri.

In addition to sharing my story in this book, I plan to launch my second solo book, 'A Poetic Summer' out into the world. One step closer to completing the four Poetic Seasons. That is definitely something to look forward to.

As this chapter ends, a picture of myself as an author emerges.

A survivor, a late bloomer, a storyteller, a global traveler, a poet, and a writer.

This is who I am, Oswald Perez!

ABOUT THE AUTHOR

OSWALD PEREZ

Oswald Perez, aka OP Writer, is a writer and a poet from New York City known for the poetry book, A Poetic Journey, Staying at Home. He has a Bachelor of Arts degree in Criminal Justice from John Jay College of Criminal Justice. When he isn't writing, he works for the non profit organization Housing Works as a donations associate.

In Oswald's chapter, a story of survival, resilience, and creativity is told. He was able to overcome all the complications of cerebral palsy to weave tales of a life being lived.

He has appeared on the podcast "Don't Keep Your Day Job". He also had his set of poems, "An American Tourist In Italy" published in the 2020 edition of the literary anthology, Groundwaters.

He is currently working on his second book of poems, "A Poetic Summer".

Connect with me:
Instagram: www.instagram.com/oswaldperez85
Visit my website: www.oswaldperez.com
My art print shop: www.society6.com/operez85
Facebook: www.facebook.com/groups/2220061314804175
Substack: oswald.substack.com/

19
RACHEL CHAMLEY

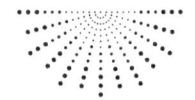

BECOMING THE LEADER OF MY LIFE

When I was asked to join this book, I started to think about courage and what it took to be a courageous human. I had never really thought of myself that way before, but I suppose I am.

I started to look back and reflect. There were many points I was courageous in my life: Playing rugby as a kid, the only girl in a team of boys. Being outspoken. Quitting my steady job to move to Zakynthos, Greece, and working in a bar. Confronting horrible bosses.

Some people would look at me and think I had no fear, that I was super confident. But I had a limit. I would follow the things that light me up, and then the internal barriers would set in. I don't know where the barriers came from or why they were there, but there was something that always stopped me from getting too happy, too confident.

Maybe it was being from a big family. Maybe it was being from a small town. Who knows, but it was definitely there. No matter how much courage I had to leap into the things I loved, I would always settle back into the sensible mode. As I got older, this sensible mode seemed to last longer and longer. I would try and fit into the normal mould. The corporate job, the marriage, the house. I mean, that's what you do, right?

I was always making two steps forward, three steps back. Constantly trying to fit in, I worked hard, long hours. I was successful and gave everything to work, but it was never enough. There was always a boss to knock me down and keep me in my place. With a strong undercurrent of 'don't shine too bright'.

I tried everything in my relationship. Constantly trying to make him happy, giving him everything, shouldering all the problems, the worries, the stresses, and yet it still wasn't enough.

Between work and home life, I finally found myself at the lowest I have ever been. At that point, I would not have known how to be courageous. I was numb, lonely, and drained. I was trapped at work with no view of how to move on, and yet some days being miserable at work was easier than being at home. Don't get me wrong, my husband loved me, I don't doubt that for a second, but we had got into such bad habits we didn't know any other way.

I tried everything to shift the numbness. Night's out, alcohol, new cars, new kitchen, new bathroom, holidays, holidays, and more holidays. Nothing worked. It was still there, and by this point, so was a mountain of debt. I knew there was something more, something I was missing, something that was going to make me happy. I could feel it. I had this niggle inside. I just couldn't work out what it was.

On the face of it, everything looked fine. I had become an expert from a young age at hiding my feelings, this wasn't hard for me. To everyone else, I was normal. Good marriage, good job, nice new kitchen. Whilst inside, I was dying. There was a part of me, that courageous me, screaming to get out.

I didn't know at the time what the courage and the niggle was. I hadn't realised it was my intuition. My internal knowing saying there is something wrong. Trying to lead me on a new path. All I knew was

I had to do something different. I had to try something new. I stumbled across a spiritual development class, and the courage leaped out of me and made me join. I had always been obsessed with Tarot readers and spiritualists. That was my go-to when I needed advice. Most people go to counsellors or therapists. Not me, I would get my Tarot read.

I loved this weekly class. It was my time out, my little bit of peace. I learned so much, and I started to connect with something bigger than me. I had always believed in fate, and that is what I thought this was—just fate. I had no clue that this was the start of something so much more.

The universe had big plans for me, and I could never have imagined any of what happened next.

I always remember seeing the phrase, "You are one decision away from changing your whole life." I would think, 'oh come on, really! It would take more than one decision to turn this shit show around.'

However, when I look back now, there was one decision that changed the whole course of my life. One instance that I can say has been that pivotal moment. It completely changed everything.

As I started to learn more and more about the spiritual side, I would share it with my friends and family. There were those who were completely for it and always keen to listen and find out more. Then there were those who thought I had lost my mind. I remember people who were into it kept saying to me, "have you watched The Secret?" "I used The Secret to get my new job." Everywhere I went, I kept seeing The Secret or hearing about it. I couldn't seem to escape it.

So, one night after a horrific day at work, I got home and poured myself some wine to drown my sorrows. I thought, 'right, I will watch it, see what all the fuss is about'. Oh my god! There it was, like Zeus himself had crashed a lightning bolt right through me. I saw the light, shall we say. Something connected deep inside of me, and the niggle was right. There was more. I had a vision of me standing on stage in front of hundreds, if not thousands of people teaching something. It was so clear. I had absolutely no clue what I was saying, but they were all stood up, loving it.

In that second, it was like a part of me that had either been buried or had never been realised was unleashed. I saw freedom for the first time. I saw life on my terms. There was something about this. It lit a fire under me. I instantly knew this was bigger than me. This was my purpose. I didn't know what I was teaching or speaking about, but I knew I had to find out more.

I woke up the next day with a whole new outlook and my vision for the future completely revamped. I had to learn more. I walked into work with a smug feeling. Knowing I was walking into the same situation as yesterday, but I had changed. I was no longer desperate to fit in. No longer desperate to get ahead. I had a new path, a new vision, and this wasn't it. It was a means to an end. How freeing.

My whole life had literally taken a turn that I wasn't expecting. All my future plans were suddenly out the window, and this new vision had taken over. Now I just needed to figure out what it meant. I dedicated all my free time to learning more about manifesting and exploring all the teaching The Secret mentioned. I took webinars, read books, listened to podcasts: I was completely hooked. Friends and family thought I had lost my mind, but I had to carry on. I had enough courage to let my intuition guide me. I was led to the right people in the right places, and I took it all in like a sponge.

It really was incredible. However, the more I learned, the more my current reality seemed disjointed. It felt out of alignment with who I was becoming. I had to make a choice. Do I apply what I have learned and follow my intuition, or do I stay where I am and carry on? This was the hardest decision of my life, but I knew deep inside where I had to go. I had to manifest my magnificent life. Sensible just wasn't for me. I couldn't mould myself back into the box anymore, it no longer fit.

To understand my decision, I will have to take you back and explain what I had learned so you know why the sensible mould would never fit again. The Secret opened my eyes to something I had never heard of before. Manifesting. This was a completely new concept to me, and it is to most people. It is the concept that we create our external world through the vibration of energy. Imagine yourself as a magnet, attracting everything around you. The quality of what you attract is based on the quality of your beliefs, your emotions, and your thoughts.

Imagine that all the numbness, all the horrible bosses, all the relationship worries, I was attracting it to myself. Not intentionally, of course, but I was. Where your focus goes, your energy flows, and I was focusing on everything that was going wrong. This just created more.

Now the main concept of manifesting is to ask for what you want, believe you can have it, and receive, by being open to the universe delivering it. Seems simple right? Well, not at first when it's all new. I had some work to do. I had some additional steps to make it all come together. Six, in fact, and I will share them with you.

1. REFLECT AND ACCEPT.

Initially, once the Zeus-style lightning bolt struck me, I was left feeling a bit overwhelmed. I needed to get my head around how I had manifested these things in my life. I realised that it was no one's fault. I had spent so long blaming bosses, my husband, and money for how I felt, and suddenly I realised it was mine. Not consciously, but what you accept, you choose.

I had accepted people treating me badly. I would let bosses' opinions affect my self-worth. That was my choice.

I had accepted the dynamics of my relationship. We had a pattern. Things would be bad, we wouldn't be getting along, lots of mood swings, or we would take each other for granted. We would finally talk about it; we would say things would change, and we would carry on. Until the next time. Again, this was my choice. I had chosen to carry on, to say it was ok.

2. ASK/ FOCUS ON WHAT YOU WANT.

I realised I had constantly been focusing on what I didn't want. All the stress and worry, I was completely lost in it all. Now was the time I had to turn this around. I had to decide what I did want, what I was going to focus on now. I had to visualise my dream life. This was so difficult at first as I had never thought about what I actually wanted. I look back, and I never used to even like setting goals. I thought they won't work; they won't turn out as I had hoped, so why bother being let down. So to start focusing on what I wanted instead of leaving things to fate was a big change. I started to see my new life. Over time it grew clearer and clearer with the vision of me on the stage being at the heart of it. I wanted to be a life coach. I had a passion for helping others transform as I had. Little did I know that it was this transformation that I would be teaching.

3. IDENTIFY YOUR BELIEFS.

This was a big one. As I started to reflect and uncover more, I realised I had a huge limiting belief that other people were better than me. This was an ah-ha moment. It had manifested all through my life. Thinking I wouldn't get jobs because the other candidates were better. Thinking my siblings were better than me. Putting my husband on a pedestal. He came first, I put his emotions first, his career first, everything. Now most women will be reading, thinking I do that, and I know it is so common. The issue is it doesn't work. I couldn't make him happy. We try and try to make others happy, but it is an inside job. No other way I'm afraid.

4. TRANSFORMING YOUR BELIEFS.

Now I had realised what beliefs had been holding me back, it was time to release them. To free myself. I had never done this before or knew how, but luckily this is where my intuition kicked in. I was led to the right people and the right places. I learned how to transform limiting beliefs through meditations, energy healing, and, most importantly, Emotional Freedom Technique (known as tapping). Tapping was a game changer for me. One session transformed that belief that others were better than me. One session! It was incredible. So much so that I decided to become a practitioner and help others do the same. Transforming this belief changed everything. Now I could finally focus on myself. I could finally step into the lead role of my own life. I had never played that part before; it was definitely time.

5. INSPIRED ACTION

I love this stage; you can have so much fun, but this is the stage I definitely struggled with at first. There is a good saying which applies. "Act as if", this is where you start to embody the new you, acclimatise yourself with the reality you want, and raise your vibration. I tried different things, affirmations, journaling, and gratitude, but I was still surrounded by the same things which made me feel as far from where I wanted to be as possible. I needed more impact. I needed things to happen quicker. I needed something to keep me committed to raising my vibration, rather than just dipping my toe in every now and again. So I started an Instagram page all around gratitude. I started to imagine people all over the world joining in (this actually came true).

Over time the journaling and meditation became daily along with the affirmations to replace those old negative beliefs. All these little things seemed so trivial at the time, so small, but they have a huge compound effect. These small degrees of change shaped my whole future, and I teach these now in my programs to clients all over the world.

6. RECEIVE

Receive. Seems easy. Mmm, not so much. Think about when someone gives you a compliment, do you say thanks? Or do you squirm and say, "this old thing?"

I was definitely a "this old thing" person. I had to change. I had to open up to the universe helping me. I had to open up to anyone helping me, and I had to be open to the universe bringing things in a different way. As someone who had always had to manage everything, a self-confessed control freak, this was a shift. There are some days I remind myself of this still.

These six steps are not just a process, they became my way of life, and everything started to change. Work improved, new opportunities arrived, the awful bosses moved, I started to enjoy my job again. I was feeling happier, more confident, and money was flowing. I was growing so much my old life and mindset seemed distant. I could see my new future, and I was going full steam ahead. This is when the courage had to kick back in.

I had parts of my old life still there, still unchanged. My husband had seen my journey, he'd seen my growth, but he wasn't at a stage to grow with me. I had a choice to make, between the sensible me or the courageous me. The sensible choice would be to stay as things were, not to carry on with this big vision and live the life I had signed up to. The courageous me wanted to see where the vision was going, to keep moving forward no matter what.

Looking back, this was never a choice between the sensible me and the courageous me. It was a choice between being the lead role of my life and giving that part to someone else. I chose to take the role. I chose to leave, to walk into the unknown, to keep following my intuition no matter what.

Your intuition will never fail you. So really there is just one decision to make, "when will you take the lead role and manifest your magnificent life?"

Looking back now, this is where I know I was courageous. I stepped into a path of the unknown. Sat looking at the person I had loved, cared for and tried to protect for years, seeing the pain they had felt as I said "it's over." Every bone in my body wanted to take those words back, to stop the pain. But my heart kept fighting, that niggle inside was now running the show and saying "no, no, you can't." I'm so grateful I had the courage to trust it, for both of us.

Without that courage and trust I would not be where I am, 3 years on. I am worlds apart from the woman I was. The niggle continues to run the show, always putting me and my happiness first which has led to me manifesting the most unbelievable things.

An amicable divorce and getting to see my ex become a father which he wanted more than anything in the world.

The most amazing, supportive, loving partner I could ever ask for.

A dream job as a Leadership Coach, with may I add, an amazing boss.

The perfect home with a sea view, trees in my garden and so much space.

Hosting my own Podcast.

Meeting so many inspiring people.

My own business. Where I support women all around the world to find their own courage and manifest their magnificent life.

And the best bit....knowing the best is yet to come!

ABOUT THE AUTHOR

RACHEL CHAMLEY

The multi-passionate British redhead Rachel Chamley is here to create an impact in this world and 'normalise the woo'. After spending her life trying to fit into corporate roles, she was left feeling drained and out of alignment with her true values. Rachel woke up to the realisation that she had been gauging her self-worth on the opinions of whichever boss she was working for at the time and, at that point, decided there had to be another way. After many years of self-exploration, she found the power was within her already, and it was time to unleash it into the world.

As a Mindset and Manifesting Coach, Rachel is now changing the lives of other women empowering them to access their own inner power and manifest their true heart's desires. She brings a beautiful blend of masculine strategy and feminine flow to her practice which empowers her clients to achieve perfect alignment whilst stepping into who they are truly meant to be.

Website: www.rachelchamley.com/
LinkedIn: www.linkedin.com/in/rachel-chamley-b73574a0/
Instagram: www.instagram.com/rachelchamley/
Podcast: podcasts.apple.com/gb/podcast/manifesting-straight-talk/id1513224311
YouTube: www.youtube.com/channel/UCVNo7FnVo6PfNgGs1IZDqrw

20
DR. KRISTINA TICKLER WELSOME

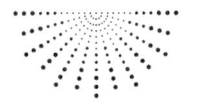

LOVE IS REAL.

DESIRING TO FEEL LOVED.

I never felt truly loved until I dared to show up as my authentic self. Our greatest wish is to be loved for who we truly are, yet we fear being open and vulnerable enough to let others in to really see us. I believe if we cannot be brave enough to show up in all of our flawed glory, then what we present is a false self to others and the world, and therefore the love or admiration we receive does not feel true to us.

Personal crisis in the form of the end of my 22-year marriage caused a need for me to re-evaluate who I was, who I aspired to be, and what I wanted out of my one precious life. I connected with the work of Danielle LaPorte and her philosophy of setting life goals as defined by the Core Desired Feelings you want to experience in your life instead of setting objective goals and accomplishments for yourself to achieve. Connecting with my core desired feelings led me to define five things I wanted to feel in my life: Joyful, Healthy (mentally and physically), Authentic, Abundant, and Love(d). Once I identified these core desired feelings, I started to use them as my north star, guiding me towards where I aimed to go in life and how I desired to feel along the journey.

What is the difference between LOVE and LOVE(d)? I struggled to gain clarity on this for quite some time. Being specific with your word choice makes all the difference. Initially, I understood being loved as love coming to me from an external source. This is something I have absolutely no control over. Seeking to "be loved" required someone or something outside of myself to provide me with that feeling instead of creating love within myself. I was encouraged to settle on being LOVE or LOVING to put the desired feeling within my control and power to create. Ultimately what my soul truly desired was to feel LOVE(d) in my life. I thought I needed that love to come from a man, as one of my greatest desires is to have a best friend and loving partner to grow with and enjoy doing life with.

That feeling of being loved did come to me in male form. Specifically, in the blessing provided by the three young men I was entrusted to raise into divine masculine men. The ones who showed me forgiveness, acceptance, care, compassion, and love when I couldn't seem to find it for myself. They have been my love, peace, and joy since the day they each arrived in my life and have always been my source of hope for better things to come. As a mother, my love for them knows no bounds. It was their love that saved me and encouraged me along this journey to find and love my authentic self.

I then realized that I was also loved by my family and friends — but I had never allowed myself to receive it due to my own internal sense of shame and unworthiness. I needed to go back to review my childhood, adolescent, and adult traumas through more merciful and experienced adult eyes. This allowed me to discover and accept who I am at my core, find meaning in my mistakes, have compassion for my perceived failures in light of my imperfectly perfect humanity, forgive myself and allow others to help and support me on my healing journey.

Incredibly, as I wrote a book about unlocking your authentic self, it dawned on me that I had somehow arrived at a state of self-acceptance and self-love as well. I was not only love and being loving—I was truly LOVE(d)... by my Self. And by The Divine as well. This transformed how I viewed myself and allowed me to start showing up consistently in my life as my true authentic self. The mask I had worn to hide and protect myself was cast aside, and I started living more courageously, despite the persistent anxiety, fear, and self-doubt that continued to plague me.

OUR OWN AUTHENTICITY IS WHAT MAKES LOVE REAL.

Courage is my word for 2021—the courage to lead with my heart, to show up with love, to dare greatly, and step into the arena of life by showing up for myself, as myself. I saved seats for my critics and welcomed them to be present. I ignored their taunts and jeers. I surrounded myself with true friends who support me, remind me who I am, pick me up, and cheer me on when I am weary from the battle. I have never been a fighter. Love is my one desire.

I connected with an incredible man. I remember feeling that my heart recognized him when we met. He was the first person with whom I felt safe and secure enough to remove the armor that protected me and be fully open, vulnerable, and completely authentic. I felt seen. I felt heard. I felt appreciated. I felt adored. I felt loved. I had feared showing up as my authentic self and being rejected for it. Instead, the totality of who I truly am at my core, with all my flaws and aspirations, was embraced and celebrated in a way that allowed me to step into and live it fully. I was finally able to truly give all of myself to a man, and in return, I received my greatest desire. To feel what it is to be loved for all that I am as a perfectly imperfect human being worthy of being loved.

While this new love experience gave me the opportunity to feel truly loved, in the end, it also brought the opportunity to face my worst fears as well. The offer of my true authentic self and love was rejected and abandoned. His abrupt about-face over the span of a day that started with, "I love you. I want to see you. I have never been happier." and ended with a totally unexpected reconciliation and return to his ex-wife by evening left me reeling and doubting all that had been shared between us. While fully trusting in his love, completely exposed and open to him, believing in the future I was co-creating with him, he walked away. He chose to follow his heart and do what was best for him. Once again, I found myself standing hurt and alone in the arena. Feeling old wounds flare up and threaten to take over my life, I found myself back in the torturous space of distrusting my own perceptions again, wondering what was actually real and true—drowning in self-doubt, feeling that the words, experiences, and love he shared with me were not real at all. The promises and future plans made between us had filled me with such joy and hope for the future. I'd faced my fears of intimacy, rejection, and abandonment because I trusted him when he told me he loved me and I was safe with him.

Did I imagine the deep connection, breathless moments, and soul-nourishing love I experienced? Can such an intimate experience be only felt by one party? Wouldn't the love need to be reciprocated to reach such a deep level of resonation? Something magical happens when you meet someone special, and you simply have to believe that the love shared was real. I'll never know what was true for him as his choice ended all connection and communication between us. However, I do have the personal transformative experience of knowing what my own reality is. Authentic love is real, at least, I know for certain that the love I gave was. I can give love because I am love, I am loving, and I am loved by myself. I showed up with an open, trusting heart, willing and able to create and collaborate on an incredible future with this man. Him walking away doesn't negate the reality of the love I gave. It also doesn't negate the fact that I remain loved and safe and secure, and I did not self-abandon.

It helps to have an optimistic yet realistic approach when you risk loving. Love, for a parent, sibling, romantic partner, friend, or child, is never easy. Love takes time, effort, and conscious commitment to succeed. The willingness to love comes with the risk of potential heartbreak. Love can often be painful. But even when it hurts, it's always worth it. I'll never regret loving or allowing myself to be loved. Unfortunately, the relationship didn't last. This beautiful life-altering experience also brought about much heartbreak, grief, and disappointment.

> "Does it hurt?, asked the rabbit. Sometimes, said the Skin Horse, for he was always truthful. When you are Real you don't mind being hurt." - Margery Williams, The Velveteen Rabbit.

Now that I've experienced the life-affirming feeling of being loved, there's no way I would ever settle for less again. Human beings are wired for connection, and I've never felt so connected to someone before. I've never felt as comfortable in my own heart, mind, body, and soul. I've never felt so expansive and in full faith of all the universe has to offer. I've never communicated and listened so easily and effectively. I've never felt more genuine and real. I've never shown up so vibrantly or courageously in my life. I've never loved more. Possibly our souls were meant to connect only so that we could each learn what we needed from each other.

"Once you are Real, you can't become unreal again. It lasts for always." In the cherished classic children's tale by Margery Williams, she illustrates how a stuffed toy rabbit becomes magically Real after being shown real love. Once you are truly loved, you feel that you become real. I believe I was able to feel and accept the love tendered to me because I showed up as my genuine and authentic self, which allowed me to accept the love given to me as true and real. To believe, for at least that moment, I was adored, cherished, and valued for my authentic self.

It's critical to recognize that it's our own true authenticity that makes us real. We should ceaselessly strive to be real and genuine in every aspect of our lives. It doesn't require other people's approval or validation to become and remain secure in who you are and to be loved by yourself. Even though the rabbit thought it was the boy's love that was what made him real, the truth is that once you wholeheartedly accept and believe in yourself, the transformation has occurred. The love of another person is simply a mirror reflecting back to us the love that we carry within us. Now that I have experienced what it feels like, I will carry that sense memory in my body and seek out opportunities to continue to love myself and hope to be loved by others in that same manner. It is healing. It is life-affirming. It is pure joy. It is what life is all about.

I am learning to love without expectation or need for anything in return. To not be attached to an outcome. To simply be grateful for all the joy and gifts he brought into my life. For the encouragement and belief in myself, he helped me to embrace. For that, all I can do is be grateful. I will continue to send him love and prayers from afar that he finds all the happiness in life he deserves.

AUTHENTIC SELF LOVE.

Being authentically connected to my own self and to Source allowed me to not self-abandon in this relationship. To remain grounded and present in the current moment. To know that, as difficult as this is, it is somehow part of the path I am meant to walk during my time on the earth. To trust that things happen as they are meant to, even when we have yet to uncover the reason why or make sense or meaning of it all. To have faith that the Universe knows what is best for me and that I can relax and surrender the situation to a Higher Power with full belief that what is meant to be will be. That what is meant for me will not pass me by. That I am loved by myself now, have always been loved by God and my family, and will be loved by the right man in due time.

Until then, I will continue to show up for myself, my boys, and those I love. I have gained more clarity about who I am and what I stand for. I know I need to be visible and present for those I serve. I am excited for what my future holds and will patiently watch to see how it unfolds for me. I know all of me is welcome here. I can speak from a non-defensive heart and continue to show who I am without fear of rejection or abandonment. I will continue to show up consistently as my most authentic self, becoming a better version every day, in full confidence that I am and will be loved.

People wish there was a guarantee in life. I, too, wish that was so, but unfortunately, there are none. No guarantees that we'll stay healthy or be happy. No guarantees that if we pledge ourselves to someone, they'll remain in love with us until the day we die. The only guarantee we have in life is how we choose to show up for ourselves, for the people we love, and in this world. Choices made out of obligation and guilt, comfort and familiarity, and fear of the unknown may cause us to miss out on the best things that ever could have happened in our life. The choices we make ultimately allow us to co-create the life we want with the assistance of the universe. No other person, amount of money, achievement, or accolade can guarantee happiness. The best guarantee we have of our own future happiness is to be in touch with our inner knowing of what truly makes us happy, to be aware of what we aspire to be in life, what we desire to have in life, and who we choose to share it with.

Being loved and loving wasn't all I thought it would be. It was actually so much more than I even hoped for. I knew there were things that I wanted, needed, and desired from a relationship. I was given things I wasn't even aware were critical for me and my well-being, and this will help me grow into the next best version of myself. I didn't know what being supported and encouraged in my dreams felt like. I didn't know alignment and soul connection could go as deep as it did. I didn't know how it would feel to be seen lovingly through someone else's eyes. I knew I came with past trauma, and I was working on letting go, yet I worried my deep fear of intimacy would keep me in hiding. I feared showing up as my authentic self. Not only were those fears allayed, but they were also proven to be completely unnecessary. In the presence of love, I learned to show up wholeheartedly and completely authentically without fear. I had complete faith and trust in this man. It's a pretty incredible feeling to have.

LOVE LESSONS LEARNED.

Love is at the very center of our being. It's the vital force that gives us energy and direction and connects one heart with another. It is irresistible attraction and affection for a person, a place, an idea, or even for life itself. Love is cherishing others, treating them with tenderness. It thrives on appreciation and acceptance. It has the power to heal. It also has the power to cause great harm when used carelessly. It causes us to continually hone ourselves while releasing the need to control or make someone in our image. When nurtured by commitment and seasoned by kindness, love has the capability to be the greatest gift we give or receive.

Without this love experience, I would not have learned to be secure in my true authentic self and the love it garnered. It showed me places to grow and expand and offered new lessons to learn so as to become the vibrational match for a love that is meant for me. Despite the ending of the relationship, it was the greatest gift I ever allowed myself to receive. I will pray and have faith that I will be given a treasure such as this again in this lifetime.

Love is bigger than any one of us. Love and the need to be loved is a basic primal human instinct that we each desire to feel. Love is something so special, it brings us great joy, fulfillment, and happiness. It is something that we want to last forever. You can't control who you fall in love with. Or whether they love you in return. We can invite love into our life, we can show up as love, but we cannot dictate how, when, and where love expresses itself. It's never easy to let go of someone you love, but sometimes the act of releasing them is necessary and the ultimate act of love for both of you.

"Love is patient, love is kind. It bears all things, believes all things, hopes all things, endures all things." One Corinthians 13.7. The practice of love is a daily practice. I choose love. I commit to love myself wholeheartedly. I show my love through acts of kindness. I allow myself to connect deeply. I accept and appreciate the ones I love. I do the work on myself that love requires. I cherish the loves of my life. Love is real. I am love, and I am loved.

ABOUT THE AUTHOR
DR. KRISTINA TICKLER WELSOME

Dr. Kristina Tickler Welsome is a Doctor of Physical Therapy, Owner of The Key To Wellness and The Key Publishing, a Holistic Life Transformation Coach, and International Bestselling Author. Decades of professional experience with patients, students, and clients makes her coaching effective, efficient, and easily integrated into your life. Her passion is to support the well-being and healing of your heart, mind, body, and soul as you learn to love your authentic self. Tina will empower you to become the author of your own life story as you discover unconsidered possibilities, remove barriers to success and unlock your full potential to live a creative life you love. Her own personal life journey prepared her to use her voice to amplify the voices of others to create even more impact in the world. You can find her enjoying living her best life as a mom of three divine masculine men in the making and expanding her own potential as a perfectly imperfect human being.

Website: www.thekeytowellness.net
Facebook page: Kristina Tickler Welsome
Facebook group: The Key To Wellness, Soul Nourishing Conversations
Twitter: Kristina Welsome
Instagram: @thekeytowellness.tina
LinkedIn: Kristina Welsome
Email: tina@thekeytowellness.net

21

VICKY LEON

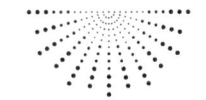

KEEP REWRITING YOUR STORY

It was a normally scheduled Monday morning meeting with my manager. Within minutes, I discovered that my job would be eliminated in 30-days. I just celebrated my 25-year anniversary with this organization. WTFudge? I felt so many contrasting emotions (and I would not cry in front of this manager); then I felt relief, relaxed, and grateful. The call ended, I took a deep breath, let a tear roll down my face, and then straightened my shoulders. It felt as if a huge burden had been lifted. I thought to myself, what the heck just happened?

I have worked in corporate for over 35 years with three global companies. This was not my childhood dream. In fact, I had no idea what I wanted to be when I grew up.

I am the oldest of three children born as first generation in the U.S., with parents and family of Puerto Rican descent. Most of my family migrated to New York in the 1950s and took on any available jobs (factory work, restaurant, house cleaning, etc.) They faced intense discrimination, poverty, language barriers, and cultural shock. Like most Puerto Rican families, mine was large, rowdy, hardworking, and did everything they could to provide for their children and for each other. We learned to be strong and resilient, along with having courage and determination. I appreciate these character traits, but I did not have direction about my future.

I loved school and did well academically. I made friends easily and engaged socially. When I was about eight years old, there was a community cadet corps that was just beginning. Some local parents decided to create this social outlet for the neighborhood kids. I had no idea what it was about, but I wanted to be a part of it! They were a non-profit youth organization, like a girl/boy scout troop, who emulated the U.S. Navy. I joined and remained with the cadet corps until I was 16 years old. We wore uniforms, learned a lot about the Navy, went camping, participated in drill team competitions, marched in parades, and had fun! I learned to play the glockenspiel and became a lead in the band. I also learned how to handle wooden rifles to participate in drill team competitions. We won several trophies!

I look back at this time and reflect on how important being a part of the cadet corps was. It saved me through some tough times (such as sexual molestation, losing our apartment to a fire, the murder of my young cousin, etc.) I believe it was in these years when *I began to rewrite my story.* Allow me to take you on a quick journey.

AN EARLY REWRITE:

In my freshman year of high school, on a September Saturday morning, I was at the cadet corps for some practice sessions. When I returned home, I saw many family members huddled in the kitchen wailing. Police had stopped by to advise that my 23-year-old cousin was found dead from gunshots. He and his friend had gone out the night before and had a disagreement which resulted in his death. As if that wasn't traumatizing itself, no one had life insurance, nor were funds available for a proper funeral/burial. Along with my family, I went out to the neighborhood, knocked on every available apartment door with an empty can of Bustelo Coffee, explaining my cousin's death and asking for donations. After many hours, over a few days, I would return home with the change we collected; pennies, nickels, dimes, and quarters had to be counted. Can you imagine? The funeral cost was in the thousands. Thank God we collected just enough. At the funeral home, the smells were overwhelming, and I thought I could see my cousin's chest rise with breath. This was such a traumatizing experience, which had a profound impact on my life. I had nightmares imagining my cousin's last moments, about me dying young and all sorts of other weird and awful things. To this day, I'm not a big fan of flowers as the smell just takes me back. So, what happened?

I had convinced myself that I would also die young, so I began to live my life with great intent. I didn't want to end up not maximizing whatever time I had left. I was only a teenager, yet my daily life was consumed with cramming lots of activities into my everyday life to not think about dying.

In high school, I became the Junior class student president and president of student government in my senior year. I was part of the dance troupe, joined gymnastics, and worked part-time at a pharmacy/general goods store. My great academics afforded me an opportunity to work as a part-time student at IBM, located on the corner of 57th Street and Madison avenue!

ANOTHER REWRITE:

I truly enjoyed working at the corporate IBM office. I felt alive being part of a fast-paced environment where everyone strived to be #1. Being hired by this company was a true privilege. If you made it here, then you were among the best. Yet, I noticed I was different: I didn't have a college degree, and I wasn't used to speaking in a professional way. I quickly realized how much I did not know. I was determined to be a part of this great organization, even though I was considered a part-time student. I dressed like my colleagues and worked on my speaking manner. I had a thick Spanish accent, even though we mostly spoke English at home. I slowed down and practiced enunciating my words.

Although I did well academically in high school, I didn't have any mentors, role-models, or counselors to help me navigate my future opportunities. Thankfully I received $1,000 from high school, which I could use towards college. I enrolled into Baruch College for a semester to test the waters. In the meantime, I was dating my husband, who wanted to marry me. I felt truly conflicted. I wanted to pursue college and a career, but I also wanted to get married. So, I graduated from high school and became a full-time IBM employee. I took the next semester off from college and got married the following June. Within a year, I was pregnant at 20 years old with my first child. We didn't plan to get pregnant so soon, but it was God's will. The thoughts of returning to college were soon replaced with being a full-time working mom. Although it was tough, I was overjoyed with being a mom to my son, and I felt lucky to continue working at the company I loved.

Work was awesome! Within a few years, I received several promotions and even won company awards and trips to San Francisco and Miami!

A few years later, I became pregnant with my daughter! I was excited about it but had no idea of the challenges we would face ahead. Both of my children were born via emergency cesarean surgeries. I was not awake for either birth, so I did not witness their entry into the world. I was initially sad about it, but with all the complications I experienced, I was more relieved they were safely born. My daughter had the umbilical cord wrapped around her neck, and it took several minutes before she began breathing. Doctors initially said she would be ok.

About 6-weeks later, we almost lost our newborn daughter due to Urinary Tract Infection. This was a very difficult time seeing our baby hooked up to so many tubes. Thankfully she recovered, and we were able to bring her back home. I was still on unpaid maternity leave, and a few weeks later, my husband unexpectedly lost his job. No warning and no severance. Christmas was only three weeks ahead, and we felt the wind knocked out of us. What were we going to do? We didn't qualify for any assistance, so I had to renegotiate returning to work early from maternity leave.

A few weeks later, during a long weekend, we travelled to Virginia to visit my brother, a naval officer stationed there. We enjoyed a lovely weekend getting away from New York City. On the drive back, the city seemed more gray, dirty, and unwelcoming. It was the first time we returned home from a trip and felt miserable. Something deep down was changing, but we didn't know what it was.

ANOTHER REWRITE:

On that Monday, I returned to work. While scrolling through emails, there was one asking for volunteers to separate from the company. For a moment, I paused. I loved working for IBM and looked forward to returning and progressing. However, my heart felt differently. I called my husband and shared the potential decision needing to be made. I submitted my name and was instantly pulled into meeting after meeting by several managers advising that I was not a targeted employee. This option was designed for underperformers or employees close to retirement. I explained that while I loved working for the organization, something in my heart was calling me to something else. Thankfully, they approved my separation with the offer that I would be welcomed back if things didn't work out.

In about 90-days, my husband, kids, and I relocated to Virginia Beach, with no employment opportunities lined up. We secured an apartment and agreed to try this new experience for one year. We believed we would figure things out along the way. *Little did we know we were rewriting our story!*

We didn't anticipate the culture shock we would experience moving from NYC to the south. We had to redefine many expectations. The job market was geared towards military and/or retirement families, of which we were neither. Finding a job that could support us was difficult. My husband eventually was hired as a customer service rep with a catalog company. Although the initial idea was for me to remain at home full time, the expenses were mounting. Our daughter continued to experience various health issues, thus I needed to return to work as well. A few months later, I accepted an administrative assistant position at a $17K annual salary (half of what I made at IBM).

The next few years were filled with my husband and I working night/day shifts to accommodate our family's needs. Honestly, it was tougher than we thought. Extremely low wages and mounting medical expenses prompted us to live on the bare minimum. Both kids settled in nicely into school and daycare while we continued to deal with my daughter's various health issues. Thankfully, there was a children's hospital about 30 minutes from the house. We were blessed by all the wonderful care my daughter received!

ANOTHER REWRITE:

Eight years later, we purchased our first home in the spring of 2001! Our son was a freshman in high school, and our daughter was in 5th grade. September 11 is my husband's birthday. On that fateful day, 9/11, his sister was in the first tower of the World Trade Center. For hours we watched the T.V. showing the horrific images of the attack and subsequent collapse of both towers. At the time, we did not know which one she worked in and honestly thought she didn't make it. It wasn't until nearly midnight when we received the call from our brother-in-law that she was alive. This experience totally shifted our mindset about life!

ANOTHER REWRITE:

In 2002, we became born-again Christians. We previously were raised as Catholics and followed all of the typical milestones (baptism, penance, communion, confirmation, marriage) and memorized all of the prayers and rituals. However, this has always been an area of contention for me. I never felt I belonged. I didn't understand why I felt I was always being told I was going to hell and that God seemed to be this angry being. Although I grew up in the Catholic framework, I always felt that I was searching for a way to get closer to God.

My sister invited me to witness her "baptism" in a non-denominational church. As a Catholic, I wasn't happy to hear this, but I knew I had to support her. Little did I know that the experience of her baptism would change my heart forever. I'm a fairly analytical and logical person. Everything about this experience made NO SENSE! We entered this building that had no candles, no holy water, and no statues. I thought, what kind of church is this? We went into a room that had a stage with a large tub. They began to sing songs of worship which really touched my heart. As they began the baptisms, each individual stepped into the tub, and the pastors would pray over them. We could hear their prayers of hope and prophecies over each person. Then, four people brought in a quadriplegic gentleman. As they prayed over him, he groaned with his response. While we could not comprehend his words, our hearts knew he was filled with joy. I couldn't believe how emotional this experience was and the impression it left on my family and me. We returned to church the following Sunday for service and were moved beyond tears. The pastor's message of love, hope, acceptance, and encouragement really left an impact. I couldn't wait until the following week to go back. Within a few short weeks, when the Pastor made the invitation to come to the altar and give our hearts to God, I couldn't run fast enough. My eyes were filled with tears of joy, and my body was filled with energy and excitement. I repeated the prayer of salvation, and my life has never been the same. Little did I know that my husband went down a different aisle and also gave his heart the same day. My two kids gave their hearts to God a few short years later. **God helped us to rewrite our story!**

In 2004 we sold our 1,700 square foot first home and purchased our 2,700 square foot second home. This wasn't even planned (there is a whole story on this for another time—lol). In 2017, as empty nesters, we sold our second home and thought we would move back to NYC. Our daughter moved into her college dorm, and our son was married and living in his first apartment. Little did we know that we would purchase our 3,300 square foot third home in 2018. God knew why we needed the larger house. There is another story behind this!

So much has happened in my life, and having a relationship with God, as a born-again Christian, has really shaped my decisions and actions. God helped me to overcome my fear of death and dying young. I decided to return to college as a working mom and completed my associate's, bachelors', and master's degrees. We discovered my daughter has several intellectual challenges which require extensive physical and occupational therapies, counselors, special education programs, and accommodations. Today she is just a few credits away from her bachelor's degree in Communications with a minor in psychology. She wants to become an advocate for individuals with similar challenges. My son, also a college graduate, is married to a beautiful woman of God, and they have a three-year-old daughter. My granddaughter is teaching me new ways of rewriting my story.

Revisiting my opening chapter about losing my job of 25-years, I decided to go on a personal journey to discover myself. I didn't know what I wanted to do and determined that I would explore different things to find myself. In 2020, as the Covid-19 pandemic began, I joined some Facebook programs, which led me to become a certified Health and Life Coach. I am currently pursuing mastery level programs and will begin my business as a Life Transformation Coach by Jan 2022.

In April 2021, my entire family tested positive for Covid-19. My daughter-in-law and I ended up in the hospital after two weeks of progressive symptoms. We were both very sick, having Covid pneumonia, and I also had sepsis. Thank God, we did not need to be ventilated, but our bodies took a beating. We were lucky to have survived and to recover. We both still feel some lingering symptoms, but we are determined to restore our health. For me, this was a second chance at life.

Today, I feel God's calling on me to pursue my Life Transformation Coaching even more so. There are so many people who could benefit from mentoring, encouragement, and coaching. With my years of management along with some life experiences, I have a big heart to offer hope and possibilities in the areas of health, finding one's purpose, changing money mindsets, relationships, and careers.

Being invited to join this amazing cohort of writers is another "rewriting of my life story." A few years ago, my very dear uncle suggested that I write a book about parenting a child with learning disabilities. I appreciated his belief in me, but I haven't been ready to tell that story. I have had several experiences, some would call serendipities, others would call them confirmations from God, which have confirmed that I should write something. I was not sure if I could do it and did not know how to begin.

Thankfully, this wonderful writing opportunity has given me a chance to share some short stories of my life's twists and turns, which helped me to rewrite my life story. I believe God isn't done with me yet, and he'll continue to guide me through the winding roads of life, taking me through more U-turns and roundabouts. I am very excited about how God will use me as a life transformation coach to help others rewrite their life stories! Thank you for reading just a few of mine!

ABOUT THE AUTHOR
VICKY LEON

Vicky Leon is a certified life transformation coach, an emerging writer, and a corporate professional. Her chapter reveals her personal journey with overcoming life's challenges, taking actions, and rewriting her life story that resulted in many triumphs! She is a first-generation Puerto Rican, raised in Brooklyn, NY and now resides in Virginia with her husband Ted, her daughter Diana, and her son and his family, David and Kalmonie and granddaughter Sophia! Her Christian faith guides her in all things.

She earned her MBA, BA, and AA degrees, as a full-time working mom. With 35+ years of corporate experience, Vicky has mentored employees, colleagues, and students to discover their strengths/successes in their jobs and personal lives. Coach Vicky's passion is to help individuals understand what they want and to teach them strategies to inspire actions, so they can actualize their own dynamic life!

Email: veleon@lifecoachvicky.com
Facebook Page: www.facebook.com/vicky.leon.71
LinkedIn: www.linkedin.com/in/vicky-leon-mba/
IG: @vickyleon.84

22
ABOUT THE PUBLISHER

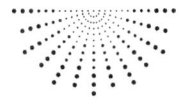

THE KEY PUBLISHING HOUSE

Dr. Kristina Welsome DPT is a Doctor of Physical Therapy, an Associate Professor of PT at New York Medical College, an International Bestselling Author and Publisher, Holistic Life Coach and Owner of The Key To Wellness as well as the founder of The Key Publishing House.

The creation of The Key Publishing House came about on her personal and professional path of continued curiosity and a willingness to learn and expand when new opportunities arise. During a difficult personal time, her own experience, therapy, self development and research led her to writing her own solo book as she searched for self love and healing for herself and her family. Becoming published herself helped empower her to improve her own life, and now she seeks to inspire you to share your story and amplify your voice to create more healing impact in the world.

Tina loves helping her clients gain clarity and get to the core of who they are and what they truly desire, set and attain life goals, remove barriers and provide tough love and endless nurturing support to help ensure they meet them!

It's time to get the coaching and publishing support you deserve to help unlock your true potential, rewrite your story and create an authentic life you love.

If you are ready to share your story, you can connect with Tina here:

Website: www.thekeytowellness.net or
Email tina@thekeytowellness.net.
Instagram: @thekeytowellness.tina
Facebook Kristina Tickler Welsome
Facebook Group: Soul Nourishing Conversations.

Printed in Great Britain
by Amazon